Additional praise for *Walking with the Wild Wind*

"Walkin' Jim is one of those rare cases; a man with a clear, uncluttered focus in life, driven by simple, profound passions. Better yet, he has had the good grace to share it with the rest of us!"

— Alan Kesselheim, author of many books, including *Water and Sky: Reflections of a Northern Year* and *The Wilderness Paddler's Handbook*

"Walkin' Jim Stoltz's book is an exploration and celebration of wildness and love and the nexus of the two. Not all of us can walk the length or breadth of America as Stoltz has done, but we can enjoy vicariously his exploits and insights."

— George Wuerthner, wilderness traveler and author of more than thirty outdoor books

"My friend Jim Stoltz walks and walks and walks in the wilderness. And like a few other famous walkers—Henry David Thoreau, John Muir, Bob Marshall, and Ed Abbey—he thinks as he walks. Now he shares those thoughts with us not just in song, but in this book. Wilderness lovers will find it very worthwhile to read these wilderness-walking thoughts."

— Dave Foreman, wilderness activist, author, and publisher of the *Wild Earth Journal*

Walking
WITH THE
Wild Wind

Reflections on a Montana Journey

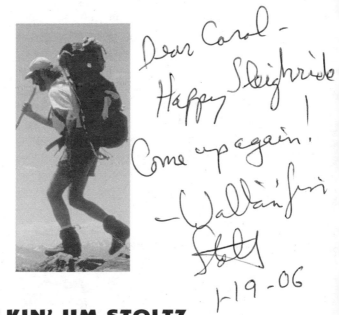

Dear Carol —
Happy Sleighride!
Come up again!
— Walkin'Jim
Stoltz
1-19-06

WALKIN' JIM STOLTZ

Cover photo: Walkin' Jim Stoltz
Photo on Author Page: Leslie Stoltz
All interior photo vignettes: Walkin' Jim Stoltz
Editing: Melanie Mallon
Design and layout: Ellen Beeler
Map by InteResources Planning, Big Sky, MT,
    special thanks to Norla Grimm

Published by Lone Coyote Publications, PO Box 160477, Big Sky,
Montana 59716

First printing, July 2003
ISBN: 0-9620228-1-0

Library of Congress Control Number: 2003093986

Dedicated to the memory of my friend,
and fellow adventurer, Lloyd Sumner.

Acknowledgments

Many people have helped this book become a reality. Lloyd Sumner read one of the earliest versions and offered me great advice and constructive criticism. Lloyd, author of "The Long Ride" and a man with numerous talents and credits, has also been a big inspiration for my life. Sandie Hancock and her reading group in Knoxville, Tennessee read and critiqued a later version. Sandie and her husband, Kevin, have supported my music and message for many years. Al Kesselheim and George Wuerthner both read my manuscript before it was edited and gave me good feedback, suggestions, and encouragement.

The process of publishing a book can be a difficult one, but working with editor, Melanie Mallon, made it much easier. Ellen Beeler has done a fine job on all the design work. I've learned much from both of them.

I've worn Vasque Boots for over 27 years. JanSport backpacks have carried my gear for 24 years. Both of these companies have been very supportive of my adventures and musical message. Other companies donating gear or products to a few of my treks have included BumbleBar, Sierra Zip Stove, Patagonia, and Cascade Designs. Dana Cordero has also provided great support by designing and maintaining my website.

This book is a product of the support, encouragement, and love of all the fans that come out to my concerts and buy my cds— all the folks who have asked me for years, "when are you going to write a book?"

My wife, Leslie, is probably the biggest reason this book project is a reality. Her encouragement and support has been steady and strong. She is the one who has urged me on and read each version of the manuscript. Leslie is my final editor, my best critic, and my biggest love.

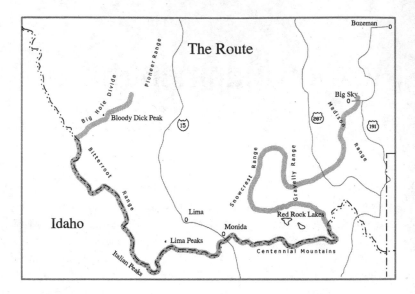

The Route

Bozeman 0

Pioneer Range

Big Sky 0

Big Hole Divide

Bloody Dick Peak

15

287

Madison Range

191

Bitterroot Range

Snowcrest Range

Gravelly Range

Idaho

Lima 0

Red Rock Lakes

Monida 0

Lima Peaks

Centennial Mountains

Italian Peaks

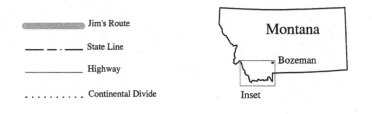

Jim's Route

State Line

Highway

Continental Divide

Montana

Bozeman

Inset

Back on the Trail Again

I'm back on the trail again,
Missed you like some long lost friend,
Sometimes I think I'm just a part of the wind,
When I'm back on the trail again.
    —from the song "Back on the Trail Again"

The little truck bumps and bounces along the narrow dirt track. I brace myself for each rattling tilt, knees banging against the dash, long legs cramped and crowded. The cool air nips at my bare legs. My shorts seem out of place at the moment. I shiver and rub the goose bumps, glad that it's not a long ride this morning and that I'll soon be moving on my own two feet.

It's early. Barely day. A faltering beam of steely morning light filters through the lodgepole pine. Leslie drives slowly, concentrating on drilling me for forgotten items in my pack. She rattles off an endless list: tent, sleeping bag, stove, fuel, cooking pot, cup, spoon,

1

matches, pack cover, camera, film, journal, tripod, books, guitar, picks, capo—it goes on and on. I answer automatically. If something is missing now, I'll just do without. I'm looking out the window, thoughts in the high country. It's a good day to start a long walk. It's a good day to go back to the wild places.

I wear the morning chill like a blanket. It makes me shiver with the cold, but also with a growing excitement. This is not my first long trek. The past seventeen years have led me over 17,000 miles through the backcountry of North America. I go nearly every year. I know the big outside well, but I've been away from it. Today I'm returning to those precious stretches of wilderness, those last places where Mother Nature still runs things. Back where the rivers are clean, the forests untouched, and the mountains condo-free. I'll return to those rare places where the Earth still whispers secrets in the wind, places where mountain lions and grizzly bears still roam. Can't we go a little faster?

Glancing at Leslie, I feel guilty for the thought. She's staying behind to work. Last summer we walked two months and 700 miles together. The year before that, we walked our honeymoon for weeks through the Grand Canyon. I don't feel bad at all about my upcoming adventure—I've gone solo most of my life—but a twinge of guilt for leaving her behind starts to play at my conscience. She has committed for the summer to a job she loves, and staying behind was her choice, but at the moment I feel like a bum.

Leslie is a people person. She loves her time in the woods and thrives in the mountains, but she also loves frequent contact with people. She works as a naturalist and guide, taking people on hikes and backcountry ski trips, sharing her great love of nature. It's fun to watch her catchy enthusiasm for the little things begin to blossom in her clients. She's good at explaining nature, but what comes through is her love of it.

I'm staring at her now. She is a beautiful woman. Not in the classic sense, I suppose, but she has a deep down, heart and soul beauty. Her gentle eyes, green and bright, never leave the road, though sometimes she tilts her head my way to emphasize her words. I answer question after question absently, totally absorbed in the sight of her, soaking it up, letting her sunny essence fill me, storing it away for the days to come.

How much I love this woman. And she must love me, though sometimes I wonder why. She sure has a lot of patience. In many ways

Leslie has given up what most women take for granted when they marry a man, that he'll always be there, day in and day out. I'm gone so much. She hates me leaving all the time. Walking here. Walking there. Driving to this coast for a concert. Driving to that coast for another. But she tolerates all the wanderings. We do have special times when we're together, but for now, here I go again. I know why she drives so slowly, just as I know why she keeps talking, filling the silence until we part.

The truck stops, and the quiet of the hour rushes in. A sweet silence. A muted whisper that touches not only the day but all who live in it. It warms and reassures, awakens as well as hushes. I get out and walk to the back of the truck, crunching footsteps the only sound for miles. The tailgate opens with a creak. The pack is waiting, lifeless and heavy. The expectation and longing I've felt for months are suddenly gone. I stare at the pack. Leslie comes around the end of the truck and into my waiting arms. I can feel her tears. She tries to make light talk, but the quiver in her voice gives it all away. Her little body feels so right against mine. What am I doing?

One last squeeze, and then another. Finally I reach into the truck and grab the pack. It feels heavier than when I first hoisted it last night, but with a grunt, I manage to lift it onto my back. That's better. Feels pretty good up there. It's a good fit, kind of a high-tech hug.

Leslie snuggles against me. We try to embrace with the giant pack looming over us. And then, with a kiss on my lips, she is back in the truck and rolling. We wave. And wave again.

I start to walk up the jeep trail, but the lump in my throat stops me in my tracks. I turn to watch her go. It'd be so easy to stay. I could give a yell right now. (*Stop! Come back!*) The truck is getting smaller. (*Wait for me! Turn around! Come back!*) But who am I fooling? Even if she does stop now, I can't. Something draws me back year after year to the backcountry. Something that fills me as nothing else can. Something that even the woman I love can't duplicate or comprehend. And how can she, when I don't even understand it all myself?

The truck glides slowly out of sight. I'm alone. This is where it starts. Right now. This is where it all begins. It's that *first* step that matters most; not the moving of feet, but the action of letting go. You see, solo long-distance hikers leave behind the hustle and bustle of our modern world. We turn our backs on telephones, hair dryers, automobiles, and all the "stuff" that clutters our lives. We leave so-called security (walls, locks, and fences) and the comforting embraces of our loved ones. Somehow we must come to grips with what we leave behind. We must swap it for something else. In turning away from the familiar world of roads and houses, we must turn toward the Earth on which we trod. In a way it is a homecoming, returning to the land and the natural rhythms that govern that land. It's also the start of a life of silence, a time of contemplation. This is a time when we absolutely must face ourselves, a time when solitude becomes a way of life. It is also a time of unpredictable adventure. There's no telling what awaits around each bend of the canyon, over each mountain ridge.

The Altar

Each time I come to this altar
I find more clothes
Left behind,
Rotting on distant shelves
Where they belong, lost
To the vision
Of what floats here alive.

Each time I come to this place
The Spirit takes me,
Deeper down
The trail over the hill
To where Truth lies
Golden in the sun,
Living
In the tracks behind
And the footsteps to come.

I turn and step out. One step, then another. The walking feels good. The jeep trail is soft underfoot. Little puddles from last night's downpour lie like tiny mirrors reflecting the shining day. The forest still holds the aroma of rain with the tangy scents of spruce needles, mud, and grass. The air hangs, freshly scrubbed and calm, clean as only mountain air can be. I soak it in, down deep in my lungs. Each step brings me closer to the wild, and closer to the peace I need. For two months I will be afoot. For two months I will walk with the wind and sleep with the stars. For two months, I will be my own man, here where it's just me and the mountains.

I walk slowly. The morning isn't something that can be hurried. It'll be gone, too, soon as it is. Why be here if not to savor each breath of air, each sound and sight? I have a week's food in my pack, and an entire world of mountains is waiting before me. The day is perfect. My body hums along, meshing with the mountain morning.

The South Fork of the West Fork of the Gallatin River roars off on my left. It's been raining steadily the past several days and, with the snow pack melting fast, the South Fork is still running high on this third day of July. Two months from now I'll descend the North Fork of this same river and complete a 700-mile loop of southwestern Montana's wild country. Ten different mountain ranges wait for me. Miles of untrammeled wilderness. Such a vast sweep of life to touch shoulders with.

I need the wilderness now more than ever. It has been a part of my life even before the long treks, always a place where I felt comfortable and secure, a place where I could go to think things out. These last months have tilted my world on end, and it's time to think things out. A dull sadness beats away in me, and it needs to be shaken out. As much as I need to get to those places called wilderness, I also desperately need to get back to a distant place inside myself. Yes, it is high time I headed for the woods. They've always been waiting for me. Even when I was a child the woods were always there, a sanctuary of peace coming from the gentle kiss of a mother.

1959—HUBBARD LAKE, MICHIGAN

I'm a skinny little kid, but determined. I've managed to dog paddle my way out to the raft in deep water. It's a milestone. That twenty feet of distance, from where I could touch bottom to the ladder of that drifting piece of security, seems like a mile. I jump around atop the floating palace, a little king waving to Mom and Dad and my big brother, Mark. They laugh at me and encourage me to jump in to come back to shore.

I hadn't put much thought into the "come back" part of my feat. But the tether holding the raft has lots of play, and now it has drifted farther away from the shallow water. The water looks really deep. And my family appears quite far away now. I think I'll stay here for a while.

I hang out on the raft for a long time, ignoring my dad's instructions to come back in. Finally, he gets tired of telling me to come back. He swims out and climbs on board. Dad tells me I can do it. He points out several times that I managed to get out here all by myself.

I know that! But it doesn't make it any easier. Dad explains that the water isn't really all that deep. Yeah, but he's the one who's six feet tall. He coaxes and nudges, begs and pleads with me to try it. No way!

All this time Mom is watching. She's paddling around in the water with her easy breaststroke, passing by us every couple minutes. It's funny: I know Dad is the one who can save me if I fall in, but I'm so glad Mom is there. I know I'd be more afraid if she weren't. I know she wants me to know she is there.

Dad finally gets tired of reasoning with me. He picks me up, and before I can even think about it, I'm in the air, bound for a big splashdown. I bob to the surface, already doing my trusty dog paddle, heading for the shore. I spot Mom standing in water up to her chest. She's got her arms out to me, a concerned look on her face. This should be a traumatic experience, but I'm so calm, I feel like laughing. There ahead is the sanctuary for this six-year-old, the rock of warm security. I know with all my heart and soul that as long as Mom's arms are there to grab me, I'll be OK.

Mom always did encourage me to be my own person. That's why I'm here and who I am. I've just spent seven weeks with her back in Michigan. The time haunts me with little images: her kiss good-bye, her waving to me from the window, the shadow of illness hanging over her, and those big arms reaching out to hug me.

That first long walk she was there, seventeen years ago in northern Georgia. She and Cousin Barb drove me the long miles down from Detroit so I could walk up to Maine along the Appalachian Trail. I was living in Vermont, had returned to Michigan to arrange my resupply packages, and was going to hitchhike down but Mom insisted that I needed a better send-off than that for such an adventure. They drove two days so they could stand and watch me go.

When I turned to look from the last bend in the trail before it disappeared into the woods, Mom was still waving.

Turning around, I look back the way I've come, almost expecting to see Mom standing there, waving, but there's nothing but the empty trail and a breaking morning.

I shake out of it and find myself atop a high, steep bluff overlooking the river. An old trail leads down to a wooded flat where a logjam will enable me to cross the roaring torrent. A few days ago, while scouting the crossing, I nearly bumped noses with a bull moose in the dense forest along the river's edge. Now I keep sharp watch on the trees below. I'm trying my best to be quiet, but every other step wants to skip out from under me. The trail is a stream of slick mud. I slip and slide my way down, leaving long skid tracks to mark my jolted passing. My descent is quick and clumsy, but I note a set of fresh elk tracks on the path, revealing the same crazy dance on his descent. I don't feel quite so klutzy.

At the bottom, I follow a worn game trail into a thicket of spruce, my footsteps lighting softly on the spongy forest floor. The moose is long gone, but each footfall bears a sense of expectation as I near the river. The water's voice talks to me now, murmuring and singing its own sweet message to the day. Soon I'm breaking from the shelter of the trees, standing on a low bank, overlooking the clear, golden water.

For several minutes I stand stone still, gazing first into the flowing crystal, then down to where the morning sun is also flowing, bursting through the giant fir and spruce and splashing upon the water with a spray of silver. It seems an act of love, this morning light, a caress from heaven for the beauty of wild Earth. The beams are warm and soothing, drawing me out of myself and into this planet on which I stand. My feet, like roots, tap down toward the sweet running river. My pounding pulse feels as if it's pouring my blood into that singing stream this moment, its waters flowing into and through me, awakening something way back in there, back where thoughts cease and feeling begins. My brain has become just another touching nerve, each sense filled with icy mountain water, drowned in the perfume of dripping spruce and flooded with dancing sunbeams.

I see movement in the misty dawn downriver. There, a tawny doe is wading into the river where the steam rises with the warmth of the light's arching rays. She stops and stands, a mystical beast in the soft otherworldly mist. Her long neck stretches majestically down, an act of pure elegance. What grace in the act of drinking.

My presence, standing on the opposite side of the river, goes unnoticed. For several minutes she sips daintily, watching the river swirl by. The picture is perfect, and I feel frozen into it. Is this what true peace is?

But time, slipping silently like a thief, always manages to tick away eventually. The doe steps out of the picture and is gone. The magic moment fades with her into the forest.

Gliding quietly through the forest along the water's edge, I come to the mass of fallen trees bridging the river. My first step onto a slick log is firm but testing. (I've not forgotten the tree trunk in Maine that broke neatly in two when I was over the deepest part of the creek.) These today are good, strong trees. The full pack makes the crossing a bit awkward. The branches, sticking out in every direction, are treacherous obstacles, snagging and pulling at me. Leaning this way and that, I step from tree to tree, generally clinging to the logs as best I can. At one point, I'm standing only inches above the racing current. The water here is deep and green. The swirling depths, spell-like, hold my gaze, chill me to the bone, and take me back to a river far away.

1976—THE BELT MOUNTAINS, MONTANA

The Smith River is running high when I get to it. The past winter has been a good one for snow, and now the river is running full and deep. I've just spent two and a half days wandering down Tenderfoot Creek, with never a thought as to how I was going to cross the Smith. It's miles to the nearest bridge, and now I stand on the bank, gazing into the dark, racing water. The cliffs on the west side of the river are formidable, but there are a couple likely routes I can take to the top—if I can just get across.

I wade in. The rocks along the bottom feel slick and tricky. The current's icy grip threatens to pull me down. I step back out, looking again up and down the river. Scared.

Stepping back in, I brace myself with my walking stick. The river attacks. As if I am a germ calling to be flushed clean from this river's system, it is beating and tearing at me with each step I take, pounding my freezing legs with terrifying ferocity. As I advance into the black water, each slow, fought-for step drops me deeper into the powerful current's grasp. Finally, I can't move.

I pour every ounce of strength into standing upright against the water. Every muscle, nerve, and thought is fighting for place midstream. To move, either forward or backward, is to give myself to the rushing river. The seconds drag like days. Lead-heavy, hard days. I can feel myself weaken. One foot starts to slip. Then the other. In slow motion I struggle to keep my feet braced. I can't. It's over. I'm going down.

My feet, my legs, my numb body are all swept away. The river tosses me down the narrow canyon. I'm a tiny bit of flotsam, helpless against the power, giving in to the miles of flowing water. Lungs gasp desperately for air. Arms flail wildly against the battering chill.

Somewhere amid the growing panic, without thinking, I cling tightly to the walking stick I've carried for the past year, all the way from the Atlantic. I'll be damned if I'll let it go now!

Somehow, I wash up on shore—still on the wrong side of the river. With the last of my strength, soaked to the bone and weeping, I crawl onto the rocks. The sky has darkened, and now a mean hail pelts my freezing body. I pull myself under a fallen tree, shivering uncontrollably, despairing and alone.

I cross the South Fork without difficulty, thanks to the logjam. A tricky ford isn't required today. For that, I count my lucky stars. Since the Smith River, an intense nervousness always comes over me whenever I face a river with some power to it. I ended up building a raft to float across the Smith all those years ago. And that was another adventure in itself. I wonder how far it floated after I set it free? Today, I will stay dry. No icy dousing. No top-heavy log raft roaring through the rapids. Just a pleasant morning walk for the first miles of this journey, which suits me just fine.

During one of my first winters in the Madison Range, I'd skied down along First Yellowmule Creek from a high camp atop Buck Ridge. Back then it had struck me as being untamed, and wild. Now I'm walking along the same creek on an old forest trail, and I wonder if the area still holds that wilderness character.

After the path leads me out of the river bottom, it immediately comes to a modern logging road. The wide swath of the graded road is out of place, alien, after coming across the free-flowing river. I know it's silly, but for a moment I almost panic. I feel like I've just stepped into a no-man's-land, a lifeless place. I frantically look for the trail on the opposite side of the road. It lies there in the grass, a firm path to reassurance and back to the unaltered world I'm looking for.

True to its promise, the trail leads me through a series of silent meadows, over gurgling feeder streams, and in and out of impressive stands of old-growth fir and spruce. Each little clearing is brimmed full of bluebells and arnica, and those not yet touched by the rising sun are coated with a husky layer of frost. In the distance, a kinglet sings its song to the breaking day. Somewhere a pine siskin is buzzing. I cross the foot of a rockslide as a pika squeaks a warning. The little rock rabbit is nowhere in sight on the field of stones, but I can hear another squeak of alarm.

I don't go much farther before I begin to see more evidence of humankind. The ribbon of overgrown trail merges with another logging road, and I soon enter a fresh clear-cut. The broken, scattered trees smell fresh, and the sap is still running from the bloodied stumps. It hurts me. I walk with head bent, faster now, to get this behind me.

I suppose it's appropriate that I experience the blight of the clear-cuts on this first day back on the trail. My life in the eighties has centered on keeping the "wild" in wilderness and instilling respect for this Earth that sustains us. I'm a singer-songwriter by trade. Folksinger is what most people call me. Over the years I have written most of my songs in, and *for,* the wilderness. The thousands of miles I've walked in the backcountry are dwarfed by the tens of thousands of miles I've driven from town to town singing for wildlands. To witness one of the major problems facing these forests at the beginning of the walk, and to feel the frustration and sadness it evokes, adds a sense of purpose to my stride.

I find the trail without difficulty where it emerges from the cut, looking surprisingly unaffected by the mess just yards away. How curious that a trail can bear such innocence. One moment I walk a skid trail, stepping over and around the debris that once was a living forest. The next moment, I'm tramping up a narrow mountain path, letting the land take hold of me again. The peace of the day trickles slowly into my sadness. Gradually, it will become a torrent that sweeps it clean.

The path leads upstream through a series of meadows and patches of mature trees. The grade becomes steeper and I stop more often.

Behind me, and to the north, the Spanish Peaks rise broader and more beautiful with every foot of elevation I gain. I use the expanding view as an excuse to stop. I use it again and again. I'm out of shape.

As I climb, my lungs huff and puff, chugging me up the slope like a steam engine. I play little games with myself, seeing whether I can make it to a distant landmark before stopping to gasp and sputter. It feels good, this working of the body. Sometimes I concentrate on my breathing, feeling its tide ebb and flow, my thin frame awash with not only the beauty of the land about me, but also the invigorating life within my own atoms and cells.

The creek splits and splits again as I get higher into the more open basin of upper Yellowmule. Patches of snow still linger, and rivulets of water wander everywhere. I tramp over the snowfields and splash through the standing water.

In the distance, I note several elk and drop into a ravine to walk toward them without being seen. When I emerge, I find a herd of nearly eighty animals grazing peacefully nearby. The wind is in my favor: I catch their gamy scent, yet not a one notices me as I put a grove of trees between the herd and me. My pack is off now. I creep to within view, watching the elk munching slowly on the new forage. The bulls stand off by themselves, away from the cows and closer to where I hunker.

A big whitebark pine, nearly six feet thick, offers me a good vantage point. I crawl next to it, peering around the sturdy trunk, the herd still unaware of my presence. An old marmot, grizzled and fat, pokes his head around the corner of the big tree to look at me. Curious, he crawls around closer, nose twitching at the strange creature lying under his tree. I watch the elk herd while grandfather marmot watches me.

The morning ticks by. The herd eats and eats. I get restless. These critters definitely need some excitement this morning. I stand abruptly, step into the open, out toward the herd, and pause. None of the elk seem to notice. I take several steps and halt. The nearest bull perks with interest. I walk toward him. Slowly, one by one, they all turn toward me. Ears erect. Eyes sharp. It takes but a few moments and several of my paces to satisfy their curiosity. With a sudden rush, the entire herd begins to bound away.

An elk is a beautiful animal. Individually, each is a picture of graceful, rippling muscle, but these are creatures of the herd, and it's as a herd that the elk's beauty starts to shine. Together, they become another branch of the Yellowmule's many streams, flowing easily and naturally across the rolling slopes of the basin. The ground rumbles and shakes with the flood of their passing while the air fills with dust and the song of their strong voices mewing and whining. In two minutes the only movement to be seen is this lone hiker making his way slowly up the side of the bowl-like valley.

The wildflowers at my feet become more abundant with each step. At first I attempt to sidestep each tiny pearl of color but soon find it impossible. The flowery carpet is everywhere. Shooting stars, buttercups, bluebells, prairie smoke, larkspur—they stretch like a sea of rainbows at my feet. At one point I drop the pack, kick off my boots, and run to this world of pinks and blues, purples and yellows. Sometimes I think that toes were made just to run wildflowers between them. How good the cold, damp earth feels against my skin.

Later, I reshackle myself to the pack and boots. The crest of the ridge is closer. The upper basin holds more extensive patches of snow. Deep but firm to the step, the drifts don't inhibit travel at all; that is, to a hiker.

Topping out on the crest of Buck Ridge, I find the little jeep road still covered with snow. I sigh with pleasure. The area has become overrun by off-road vehicles and ATVs (alter-the-terrain vehicles) since it was left out of the bill designating the Lee Metcalf Wilderness several years back. I'm pleased to have it still shut to the noisy machines by the lingering snow. Today the ridge will lie untrampled in peace and quiet.

The gnarled whitebark pines along the ridge's edge stand weathered and battered by their seasons in the high country. Like wizened old men, backs stooped by years of snowy burdens and heavy winds, each tree is a monument to tenacity. Even the fallen ones lie with majesty still intact, their woody skin polished smooth by the mountain elements. Walking amid the white bark is like walking through a museum, but here the brush with the ages is with a living part of the great outdoors.

Buck Ridge is a wide flat-topped ridge, fringed in trees, possessing one of the most beautiful mountain meadows in the region. I step into the vast clearing, which is alive with thousands upon thousands of glacier lilies and spring beauties. The flowers are everywhere, nodding crowns stretching into the distance and spilling to the foot of looming, whalelike Sphinx Mountain, which peers over the ridge to the west.

The Sphinx is a landmark from any direction. Named for its Egyptian twin, the mountain raises its sharp walls and majestic head with a noble air that demands attention. Its image draws the eye and holds it. The mind may wander but is always lured back to contemplate this towering wave of rock. With monolithic proportions and grand, striking lines, the peak stands out as a mountain among mountains.

I set the pack down against a weathered gray snag, and begin a wandering exploration of the open ridge. It's hard to resist spreading my arms and singing, "The hills are alive with the sound of music. . . ." My head is light. I'm walking like a drunk, giddy with the vast views and the scent of a million flowers. The freedom of the wild places is filling me. It started this morning when I first hoisted the pack onto my back. With every mile and every sight and smell it has increased. Like an eagle spreading its wings to catch an uplift, I have opened my heart to catch this special breath of freedom.

Back to my pack, I gobble a snack. God bless the Snickers bar! Not too bad. I'll have another. Ten minutes later I stuff five wrappers into my pack, hoist it up to its lofty perch, and amble across the meadow toward a distant trail marker. The trail leads me through scattered old whitebark pines, down to an open pass, then up and over a steep snowbank to the crest of a narrow, fairly flat ridge. I'm only a few miles from Lizard Lakes, my first day's destination. It's time to stop for lunch.

With the pack propped against a big pine, I can use it as a back rest. My little guitar is soon in my hands, and a song spills forth. My fingers find new chords on their own, and a tune floats to me on the sun's rays.

This life is so rich I can taste it,
And I've given my heart to the wind,
When that rain falls down, and the sun rolls round,
I'll be thinkin' like a mountain once again.

I sing it again. Today life tastes like wildflowers, snowy peaks, and mountain meadows.

Later, I find fresh tracks—a black bear sow with a cub. My route follows their winding path, each print a treasure of its own, each curve, pad, and claw a signpost of their passage. Perhaps there's a chance for a sighting. My pace picks up.

Their trail reads well. Here, the cub wandered astray. Curious little guy, or delinquent kid? There, the sow turned over a few rocks. *What tasty treats do we have here? Now where did that cub go off to again?* The sow crossed a snowfield here. The tracks suddenly seem much larger, and even fresher, but when they step into a lush field of shooting stars, I lose them in the waving color.

A half mile later, I'm descending from the ridge, sliding down a snowbank, crunching down the rocky path toward one of the Lizard Lakes. It's not a spectacular lake. It's shallow and small, kind of marshy around a couple sides. You can't boat on it. No water-skiing here. No crowds on the beach. No beaches. My kind of place.

I've been here before. Camped right there, down where that patch of snow is. I take off the pack and wander about without it, looking for a good flat spot to sleep. A place under one of the big pines looks inviting. No need for the tent tonight. Soon the pack is propped against the tree, ensolite pad rolled out, boots slipped off, and I'm leaning against the pack, cozy. Ahhh! I stare at the big limbs hanging over me. A gray jay, head tilted, is peering curiously down at me. No food for you tonight, you little beggar! How do they always find my camp?

It feels good to lie down, relax. I'm more tired than I thought. Funny how that creeps up on you all of a sudden. I came only twelve miles today, but it was "the first twelve miles." Those first ones are always longer than the miles waiting a few weeks ahead. And I've been such a slug lately. Of course, being back East took a lot out of my sails.

I wonder what Mom's doing tonight? Probably just finished watching TV. My sister, Lisa, is helping her to bed about now. Be time to fill up that I.V. again soon, just before she hits the hay. That was one of my little jobs these past seven weeks. Fill the food bag, fetch the water, bring the medicine, watch my mother die. Helpless! Me, not her. I watched her. Cared for her. Talked with her. Cried for her. She grew stronger and more positive with each day. I'll beat it, she'd say.

This cancer stuff doesn't have a chance. Go ahead and do that walk. I'll see you in the fall. She waves good-bye to me from the window.

Under the pine, the stillness is full and complete. The only sound is the falling of water pounding down the cliffs from the snowbanks to the lake. I should rinse out my socks, cook some dinner, find a spring for water, perhaps play a little music. Or perhaps just sit here a while longer?

My journal comes first. Every day and every night on the trail, before dinner, before the clean socks and further exploration, this is a personal ritual that goes back nearly twenty years, as long as I've been doing these walks. Let's see, I did the first walk, the Appalachian Trail, in '74. Geez, where do the years go?

The AT. Anyone who's ever walked it knows what those two simple letters mean. Two thousand miles following one trail. Two thousand miles of mountains, forests, and flowers. Two thousand miles of walking. And growing. And learning. The University of the Appalachian Trail. I graduated with full honors, Georgia to Maine, class of '74. Atop Mount Katahdin after six and a half months of hiking, I searched my pockets, and then my pack, and I could find only one penny. One tarnished, tiny penny to my name—my entire net worth.

I'd started that first trek as a skinny, shy introvert of a kid. I finished as a skinny, shy introvert of a man. It had changed me. How can six months out in the mountains do anything but? I had become much more confident in every aspect of my life. I was still shy, but not painfully so. I could talk to anyone with an assuredness that made me marvel. Before the trek, that was not the case. It was a rite of passage, a quest that had matured me. Most of all it gave me a great strength, a knowledge that I could in fact do it. And that I could probably tackle anything if I set my heart and mind and soul to it. Did I gain confidence? Well, yes. Confidence with a dogged, gritty determination.

The AT was the siren that lured me on to other things. Looking back, I can see that it was one of the easiest hikes I've ever done. I didn't know it at the time. Hiking was, and always is, a great adventure, and the AT hike was my first great adventure. As the two quarter-size blisters on each heel began to heal a couple weeks into the hike, I realized I was hooked. This was where I belonged. I was totally, absolutely, completely, unequivocally into it. As the trail's end drew closer in New England, I began to slow down. Let's do a six-mile day today. Or perhaps an eight. No more fifteens and twenties. Maybe I shouldn't hurry this ending thing so much. After all, when it's over, it's over.

Somewhere along the AT, I realized that maybe it didn't have to be over. Maybe I could do another walk. I'd had dreams of Montana since I was a sixth grader, and there were vast stretches of public land out there to hike. Maybe I should just walk to Montana. A seed was planted.

The thought grew into reality: a coast-to-coast backcountry hike that led me nearly 5,000 miles over a year and a half of walking, through all seasons and all kinds of country. Afterwards, folks started calling me Walkin' Jim, and then I walked the Continental Divide, Mexico to Canada. And the Grand West Trail, Mexico to Canada. Oh, and that Arizona to Montana walk through Nevada and Idaho. And the Bob trek, the summer in the Bob Marshall Wilderness. Can't forget that year Leslie and I redid all of Colorado on the Continental Divide. That was a great hike.

Nearly 17,000 miles. I guess by now you could say I'm hooked. I never get tired of being "out there." Sure, I have my tough times, the scary ones, the stormy ones, the buggy ones. But that's all part of the trip now. Walking in the wildlands truly has become my life's work. My music springs from these places. The tunes flow from the mountain brooks, and the lyrics are caught up in the desert wind. All I do is go out and find them, write them down, and borrow them for a while. My salary is not only the concert fees and record sales but also the vast wealth I gather in sights, smells, and feelings of the last wild places. There is an inestimable value in wilderness that cannot be put into dollar signs. Can we put a monetary value on love? On beauty? On life itself?

Yes, I have made it my living, and in the true sense of the phrase. I'm lucky for that. It's been a long trail from the AT to here, but it led, and I followed. The trail goes on and on, looping back and skirting around and up, but always onward. The wimpy kid at Springer Mountain, Georgia, is gone for good, but the man I am now is, too. Each trek bends and molds me anew. I feel more full, more complete, with each dose of the wild country. Today I've felt that fullness start to blossom, but a weight holds down the edges. A pocket of sorrow walks deep inside of me as I scribble my thoughts into my journal.

After writing for a while, I stand up and stretch. Two mule deer spook behind me and trot off over the hill. I hadn't seen them. My surprise is total. I walk down to the lake's outlet and rinse out my four socks: two thin white ones, for against the skin, and two thick wool rag socks over those. Another ritual. At the end of each day, I'll rinse out the dirty socks, so the following day I can wear clean pairs. Any socks that haven't dried overnight will ride the top of the pack. Occasionally, I'll use some biodegradable soap and my cooking pot for a more thorough washing.

Once the socks are drying in the sun, I walk slowly up the hill above my camp, rope in hand, looking at the trees. I study each limb, finally finding the right one. The food will be safe up there tonight. This is grizzly bear country, and it's silly not to take simple precautions. I've never had a bear in camp, and I don't want to start now. I tie one end of the rope around a fist-sized rock and, after a few tries, get it thrown over the point on the limb I want. The rock is hefty enough to pull the rope back down to me. I untie it and let the line dangle. After dinner, I'll hoist up the food bag.

My stomach is squawking at me, but before dinner, I want to find a good water source. There is plenty of water in this Montana high country. Most is clear and pure, but with the increase in backcountry travel, some of these innocent-looking streams aren't as safe as they first appear. Giardia, tiny creatures with a giant wallop, dwell in such places and can infect a luckless hiker with a most disastrous case of diarrhea and megafarts, which doesn't sound like much fun.

There are a number of filters on the market now, and Leslie and I own one, but I didn't want to carry the extra weight on this trip. When I'm by myself in the mountains, I rarely do. Instead, I'll search out the local springs. If I can get the water from the source, from where it comes out of the mountain, the odds of picking up such a bug are greatly reduced. If I can't get it directly from the spring, snowmelt or a high stream are probably still safe. If not from these sources, I usually boil it. This is just my own feeling about finding safe water. So far it has worked.

The ridge looming over the west side of the lake is laced with tiny rivulets of water, creating a symphony of bubbling murmurs, choruses, and splashes. I wander around the lake, water jugs in hand, gazing at the marsh marigold, globe flowers, buttercups, and glacier lilies, leaping the tiny brooks that feed the lake. On the hillside I pass two small springs and follow the sound of a real gusher to a place where I fill the bottles with water so cold it hurts my throat to drink it.

Back at camp, I pull out my little backpacker's stove. Soon the water is boiling in the one pot I carry. I pull out my dinner and smack my lips in anticipation. My first dinner back on the trail. Being truly a creature of habit, I prepare the meal that starts off every long walk of mine, the favorite of nine out of ten long-distance hikers. It's easy to fix, just boil and add—my kind of recipe. It's also a great carbo load. Tomorrow, as I climb up and down the mountains without a trail, my body will be fueled off this one-pot meal. It's cheap, too. Only nineteen cents on sale at Safeway. And it's so tasty! Out here, anyway. Funny how it never appeals to me at home. What would a hiker do without macaroni and cheese?

Dinner is over. I ate too fast. My belly is bloated. I waddle up to the rope, hang the food bag, and take a short, meandering walk. The sun has gone over the ridge, but there's still lots of light. Everything is still. The lake is smoother than any glass I've ever seen. In the marsh to the south of the lake, the two does have returned, grazing peacefully.

I feel as though the Earth itself has given me a welcome hug this day, the first one on the trail. I am back. Have I ever left? The time away from the wild country often seems a blur. Things get so rushed, so complicated, senses blinded and feelings shuttered—not totally, but hobbled nonetheless. Today, I feel windows opening, doors thrown wide. It's so much easier to laugh out here. To cry. To love. To think. Here it's so easy to live. So easy to simply be.

It's cooling off fast by the time I return to camp. I crawl into my bag, sighing and relishing the warmth and coziness. What luxury I give myself. Surely there can't be a more comfortable combination for sleeping than a down sleeping bag atop an ensolite pad spread over a bed of pine-needle–strewn earth.

The stillness cradles me. The only sound is that of the distant falling of water. The light dims and fades. The limbs of the big pine begin to bear fruit. First one star, then another, is suddenly visible and hanging in the twisted arms of the big tree. Soon the tree will be ablaze, bearing the weight of an entire universe and its vast light. I won't see it. I'm already asleep.

Following the Rainbow Trail

I guess I've been a dreamer,
I'll admit it all along,
But if I didn't go chasin' them rainbows
I wouldn't be singin' these songs.
    —from the song "Following the Rainbow Trail"

Like a curtain swinging open, the new day begins. Night gives way to morning with the opening of one eye, then another. A thick layer of frost coats the meadow. It's cold out there. I burrow deeper into my bag, savoring the comfort of it all. We can't rush into things now. Better let the sun come and warm things up a bit.

I wonder what Leslie is doing. Probably up already. She loves these early hours. I do too, but she's nearly always up and about before I am. We are probably a strange couple. Most folks find it hard to understand a relationship that puts us in separate places for a good portion of each year, but even with all the times apart, it's amazing how much we've grown toward each other. Even when I'm on the road two thousand miles away I still think of her and smile at her little mannerisms. She'd be teasing me right now if she knew I was still lounging in bed. And I'd love it, but I'd better get up.

How I wish I could just crawl out of the bag and walk on my way, as the bears do it. Too bad we have such a call for breakfast and such. Not to mention all this stuff I load onto my back. There's a laugh. There was a time when we humans didn't need all this baggage. We walked much closer with things back then. I'm thinking about aborigines while I pack up, munching on a handful of granola. After a quick swipe at my teeth with the toothbrush (simply can't start the day with dirty teeth), I'm off and walking.

The trail leads me through beautiful meadows and scattered forests. Snow still lingers in the shade of the trees. The day is still, and the skies are clear. I walk softly, expecting to see a critter in each meadow I pass. Maybe a coyote or a grizz. Surely an elk, or a moose. But all I see are a thousand and one glacier lilies, dewy spider webs glistening in the sun, chattering squirrels, and a startled owl.

I'm cruising now on a perfect downhill path. No puffing here. I'm eager to descend to the low point on the ridge so I can start the long climb up to Shedhorn Mountain. My legs are on autopilot. Full steam ahead. Butterflies leap from my path. Squirrels scramble wildly out of my way. Speed limits are ignored. All the lights are green. Go! Go! Go!

EEEERRRCCCHHH! The brakes squeal. Red light. Red light! Feet dig in. I stagger to a stop and back up.

The tree on my right is covered with deep gouges, scratches deep in the bark, resin oozing from the fresh wounds. Grizz sign. Each claw mark a couple inches from the next. Long swipes, indicating a big bear. A backcountry billboard, bold as any neon. Welcome to grizz country. I walk on a little slower.

1979—SCAPEGOAT WILDERNESS, MONTANA
I break into the open meadow, stepping with relief from the dense forest I've been fighting through for the last hour. Falls Creek gurgles a promise. I walk toward it. My throat is dry, my thoughts on the cold, clear water I know is there.

Movement downstream. I freeze. A large bear steps out of the willows a hundred yards away. It's a grizz. My stomach flops. Heart thumping like the pounding creek. All in seconds, the bear turns and gallops away down the meadows, sun reflecting off silver fur and rippling like water over flowing muscle.

He's gone. I breathe again. My first grizzly bear.

At the pass, I leave the beaten track and begin following an old, partially downed wire fence. It leads me along the wide crest of the Gallatin Range across patchy remnants of snow, through cool stands of spruce, and across silent sunny clearings. This is easy walking and stunning in its beauty. The woods here are full of big trees. The small openings are dense with a thick, lush carpet of grass dotted with columbine, prairie smoke, and green gentian.

The ridge takes an upward turn. In one of the larger clearings, three bull moose graze tranquilly. The two old-timers of the bunch can't see me, but a fine young bull stands his ground, studying me as I lower my pack and dig out the camera. I snap away for several minutes until the stick propping up my pack slips. The load drops with such a loud thud that the dominant bull comes running over to see what's going on. He's a big old guy, looking all the larger from just twenty feet away. Moose don't see too well, but he takes just a moment to decide he doesn't like my looks and leads the other two into the forest at a gallop. Returning to the pack, invigorated by the sighting, I continue up the spine of the range, the image of the old bull clear in my store of memories.

1986—Cedar Mountain, Madison Range, Montana

Three bulls! Where'd they come from? They weren't there ten minutes ago. My camp is in a grove of whitebark pine on the edge of a large meadow. I've just looked up from writing in my journal to see three bull moose grazing peacefully nearby, as if they've been there for hours. In slow motion I set the notepad aside and move to my pack. My camera in hand, I round a huge tree, the last bit of protection between me and these tremendous animals.

They're huge. I edge closer, camera up. Each time their heads go down, I inch forward. The big tree at my back is always in my thoughts.

My safety valve. These seemingly gentle beasts have been known to stomp a human to death, and there are many outdoorspeople who have been handily treed by a moose with a bad temper. I'm moving carefully.

Now I'm midway between tree and moose, about twenty-five feet. All three raise their heads as one and eye me curiously. I've stepped into their space. Two of them step closer for a better look. I click a picture. Then another. Big ears twitch. Eyes stare. I begin talking softly. Words of pure mush. Romeo wooing Juliet. It works. They relax. One of them bends his giant head down to resume grazing. The others join him.

For a good fifteen minutes I watch them, talk to them, all from my frozen position, but then I begin to feel cramped. Time to go finish today's journal entry, so I turn abruptly to return to my camp. Stupid move. It's a rude movement, without thought, and out of place. It's also enough to startle three humongous bull moose.

They jump. A quick, nervous, shaky kind of jump. Their motion in turn startles me. I leap into the air, turning in one wild move to come down facing them, legs spread wide, arms open like I'm some Montana sumo wrestler. Three large moose return to earth at the same split second, legs all askew, eyes bewildered, the hair on their backs standing straight up.

All four of us freeze, hunched over and expecting. Staring at each other. Anxious. Waiting.

Five seconds pass. Then ten. A minute creeps by. A chuckle, from me. One of the moose lets out a lung full of held air. Another one sighs. I step back softly, with more respect. The moose turn away, returning to their grazing.

The old fence disappears as the pitch steepens. I'm following old blazes up Shedhorn's open east side, spooking a few elk on my way. In a clearing a half-mile below lounge a couple dozen more elk, some with calves. I begin a traverse to the north, hoping to find a more gentle approach. Soon I'm kicking steps into the hefty remnant of last winter's cornice, topping out on the ridge.

Shedhorn! What joy to finally reach this distant place. The snow is left for a wide field of color; flowers are everywhere. I'm breathless, and not from the climb. The grandeur of Montana lies before me; mountains march from horizon to horizon in every direction. The Grand Teton is visible a hundred miles away. I'm looking right into the heart of the Madison Range now, straight into the Taylors, where my route lies. I'm also in the only designated wilderness of my entire summer-long trek, the Lee Metcalf Wilderness.

I suppose I should explain the nomenclature of wilderness. Designated wilderness areas are lands that have been protected by an act of Congress. These areas of protected wilderness lie in national forest lands, some national parks, Bureau of Land Management (BLM) lands, and public properties in general. Not all national forest and BLM land is protected. In fact, most of it is still open to road building, logging, mining, grazing, and other extractive uses, which are not good for the land's long-term health. Still, with all the impacts of our modern world, there remain some wild places too remote to be developed, such as public lands that have not been designated as Wilderness by our political leaders, pristine lands where nature still functions, uninhibited by the ways of humans, spectacular areas that for years have managed to avoid the path of development and destruction.

This summer most of my hike will be in undesignated wilderness, the places that are now a point of contention between concerned citizens and industry. The timber industry wants to put roads into some of these areas. Big oil wants to develop the oil and gas fields they think they might find under some of the wild places. The livestock industry wants to continue the low grazing fees and the practices of the old days when they could put cows and sheep nearly everywhere on the public domain. And some of us would like to limit these uses and instead focus on what is good for the land itself.

With each passing year more people are beginning to see that protecting these last wild lands as wilderness is a move that preserves not only nature, but also part of the human spirit. When Congress passed the Wilderness Act of 1964, it was a visionary move. Wilderness is many things to many people, but through legislation it has become a place "in contrast with those areas where man and his own works dominate the landscape, . . . an area where the earth and its community of life are untrammeled by man, where man himself is a visitor who does not remain." The Wilderness Act was our way "to secure for the American people of present and future generations the benefits of an enduring resource of wilderness."

Today I think of those words in the Wilderness Act: "where the earth and its community of life are untrammeled by man." Here in

Montana we have over six million acres of national forest lands that fit that description, yet because of political reasons, they have not been declared Wilderness. They are the source of our clean water, the home of our vast elk herds, the last stands of superb quiet and beauty, yet our leaders still neglect to protect them. I often wish I could take some of our politicians on a long trek high into the wild country and let them feel what wilderness is. For although Wilderness now has a legislative definition, the true essence of wilderness is something that lies in our hearts and souls.

Atop Shedhorn Mountain five ravens swoop and soar around me. I'm drawn to them. Can't take my eyes off their sleek, jet-black forms playing with the wind. They don't seem to mind my presence, where I've settled myself down on the crest of the open ridge. Occasionally one or two will land nearby, then launch themselves off the steep east side and let the air carry them up and around. What fliers! Their croaks of joy carry easily this morning.

The crest of the ridge tilts gradually upward to the south. When I reach the high point, I'm flooded with the sweet scent of phlox. The clumps of tiny white flowers litter the open ridge like patches of snow. Totally absorbed by the panorama before me, I poke along for the next couple hours, through meadow after meadow, content to meander rather than "hike."

When the ridge bends west, looming abruptly into No Man Ridge, I drop steeply off the crest to the east toward Tumbledown Creek. Lots of elevation lost here, but once in the basin I'm able to follow game trails and stay above the bottom, heading toward the upper part of the canyon. The mountainside here is covered with whitebark pine and dotted with little clearings. In one I find fresh bear scat, a huge pile. Nearby is a patch of fur. Silver tip. I look over my shoulder, not feeling quite as alone as I felt before.

1981—MISSION MOUNTAIN WILDERNESS, MONTANA

I'm exhausted. I've been following the jagged crest of the range, squeezing my way through rock chimneys, pulling myself up vertical walls, and inching my way along a series of narrow ledges, all with a full pack. The beauty of the place is complete, but the travel has been difficult. Now I'm in a small, partially wooded pass. My pack is off, as are my boots. My feet are up, and I'm leaning against my pack as if it were a throne. I doze and let my upper body slide down to the Earth.

I don't know how long I sleep, but when I awake I find that I have a perfect view of the bluest of skies. For minutes I just lie there staring at the blue, trying to pierce it with my sight. As if enchanted, I can't take my eyes from it. Perhaps if I look at it long enough that color will stay with me, become a part of me.

All this time, nearly the entire day so far, I have felt alone. I've had the mountain to myself, and I've reveled in the solitude. But now, as I lie on my back gazing at the sky, I suddenly feel self-conscious, as if I'm no longer the only one here on the ridge. I don't feel danger, just that I'm being watched. I tilt my head back, and the world is upside down. Hard to tell if anything unusual is there. I'm not used to looking at the world from this perspective. I marvel at glacier lilies nearly touching my eyebrows, shooting stars so delicate they could be made of ceramic, and a few scattered trees holding "up" the Earth.

I'm about to roll over when I see it. A bear face. Over there next to one of the trees. Then I do roll over onto my stomach, eyes never leaving the distinctive features of the adult grizzly bear.

How can someone feel so secure, so peaceful and safe one moment and totally vulnerable and afraid the next? Nothing has changed. I imagine the bear has been there a while watching me, and I never knew it. Yet as soon as I see the bear my heart begins pounding and my palms sweating, perhaps because of the position I find myself in, lying there sprawled on the ground and barefoot. If this bear wants to bother me, nothing would stop him. Come and get it!

I don't know how long we share the pass, the bear peering curiously from beside the tree and me flopped on my stomach like a beached trout. I try to close my eyes and ignore him. At least he doesn't seem aggressive. The seconds tick into minutes, and the bear moves out from behind the tree, sniffing at the glacier lilies. If I were asleep it would be easy not to move a muscle, but now being conscious of trying not to move, I almost scream with the longing to stretch my legs and prop my arms.

Eventually my bear friend wanders down the mountain and out of sight. I lie there for another minute or two and then ease onto my feet. Within minutes I'm back on the jagged crest of the ridge, bound for the next pass to the south.

I'm walking the way I always walk in bear country—as if something bigger out here might want to have me for lunch. This is a rare perspective for a human. Only in grizzly bear country have I felt so much a part of nature. So vulnerable. So much a part of the food chain. It's frightening but also enlightening. We humans tend to get a bit uppity, sometimes even pompous, in our relationship to the environment. To realize that we're not the gods of the Earth, not the masters and controllers that we picture ourselves to be, is a lesson in humility we all must grasp if we are to survive as a species.

1980—Granite Park in Glacier National Park, Montana

Rob kneels over the tracks we've been following the last mile. The fresh snow crunches as he squats to study the print. Each pad and claw stands out sharp and clear as if we were looking at the paw itself. Rob reaches out, his hand dwarfed by the sculptured imprint before us, and caresses the track. It's as if he can't believe that such a huge thing could be made by one creature's passing.

"Boy, Jim, these are the freshest tracks I've ever seen."

"Yeah, I know. He's standing right over there."

The bear just appears. He isn't as large as I thought he would be; he's only about the size of five German shepherds! His fur looks scruffy. He looks agitated. Rob and I stand together, trying not to look directly at the bear. The bear begins to circle, and I'm thinking, "This guy can kill me if he wants." I'm scared, but the fear is full of thrill, too. I've seen several grizzly bears around the park this year, but always from quite a distance. A safe distance. I don't feel safe today. Here, I'm part of the scene. Part of the entire web. It can go either way.

"What shall we do?"

"Just stay put. No direct eye contact." I'm talking as if I know what to do. (Don't panic, but run for your life!) I'm glad Rob is here with me. I wonder if I could outrun him.

The bear is walking around us. Head down. He doesn't look our way directly, just glances over every few steps. Not pausing at all, he does an entire half circle, two skinny humans at the center. I'm not aware of anything but the bear. The snow, the sharp bite in the autumn air, the slight breeze, the mountains of the Continental Divide looming above us—it's all gone. We've slipped into a silent void as we watch the bear pace across his turf. I can hear his breathing and the soft mush of his steps in the snow.

The bear continues his nervous march around and over a lip of earth, dropping quickly out of sight into Bear Valley. A collective sigh from Rob and me. We're strung as tight as young bows can be. The release comes in a flood of chatter as we continue up the mountain, reliving those moments over and over.

Later, on the way down, we stand again where we had stood as the bear had skirted us. We pace out the distance between his tracks and ours. Forty feet. Close enough for me.

I'm walking softer than I did yesterday when I started. A consciousness walks here that is not present unless I'm in bear country, an awareness and alertness, unbidden, without thought. The mountains are just as beautiful, the peaceful times just as serene, but my instincts are alive, flowing, and allowed to function. Here, I thank the bear. I thank him for bringing me this feeling, for awakening the real human animal that has been hidden and buried under the tame existence I've been living.

Grizzly bears. When the last one is gone, part of our most inner selves will go too. Who will be left to humble us? Who will spark that feeling we've lost in becoming "civilized"? Who will bring us back to being a part of the Earth rather than mere riders on the planet?

My route leads me to a craterlike basin that holds a green treasure of a lake. The basin sloping up to the south is still laced with drifts of deep snow. Creeks tumble over rocky slabs at every turn. A waterfall empties into the little lake. The peaks jut into the dark clouds, and the afternoon sun tilts through them, sending a warm, eerie light over the entire basin. It's a scene of all-encompassing glory.

But the lake's outlet intrigues me. The water roars out of the northeast corner of the tarn, goes about twenty yards, and drops out of sight, rushing into the hill I'm standing on. The water pours endlessly into the mountain, smoothly, like a writhing snake slithering into its waiting den.

I wonder what it would be like under the moraine, swimming under the mountain of rock, bound for a distant patch of light a canyon away. I grab a twig and toss it in. Then another. Their disappearance only strengthens the hold the whispering stream has on me. The water calls to me. I'm so tempted to jump in and float like the tiny sticks, to the edge, dropping beneath the rock. How long would it be before my body found that spot of light? How would the rocks feel against my cold fingertips? Would I jam fast amid the sifting earth? Would I fossilize and become just another rock to hold up the hill? Another wall for the creek to wear down and carry to the sea?

A good camp spot is waiting up the ridge on the other side of the lake. I know the spot is good because I can see mountain goats. They're grazing on the cliffs like little white clouds floating over the gray rock. Their presence is a good sign.

1986—BOULDER RANGE, IDAHO

Knees wobbly, lungs bursting with effort, I have to stop. I clutch the base of a stunted subalpine fir, balancing precariously on the steep slope, far above the tiny creek I was walking along just an hour ago. My legs feel like rubber. My entire body is shaking. I can't get enough air into my lungs. I lean my head on my arm and try to relax. My body calms down, but my thoughts can't. I'm in a tough spot and know it.

This is Idaho. The Boulder Range. And I'm trying to get to the east side, over the crest, without a trail. I thought it'd be an easy bushwhack over the ridge, but when I was down below I couldn't see the ledges and cliffs that would block my way.

I'm strong. I've been walking for almost three months. But this is steep. I really shouldn't be here. One false move, one slight slip, and I'm a goner. No one knows where I am. No one would ever know. Maybe I should try to turn around.

I'm looking above me, to the sides, everywhere, trying to find a route that looks halfway doable. Let's try for that next little ledge. Maybe I can see something from there. I let go of my little anchor and labor over another shelf of tilted rock. Reaching the spot I'd seen from below, I stop again, trying to catch my breath. The seconds pass. Again I look upward. A movement catches my eye. A white patch of snow seems to be moving across a barren brown shelf. Snow? No. It's a goat. A mountain goat.

What relief. Another living being is here on these scary slopes. I'm not alone. A goat! Suddenly I'm not afraid. My strength returns. With it, my confidence. I head toward what looks like a wise old billy. I'm sure he sees me. Between the steam-engine puffing of my lungs and the scrambling through the rocks, I'm traveling with all the grace of a garbage truck but he doesn't run. I've seen these goats travel fast when they want to. He could be a mile away by now. Instead, he stays just ahead of me, making his way up the precipitous slope, stopping to look back down at my snail-like progress, then, as if assured that I will follow, slowly returning to the climb.

For almost an hour the goat leads me through a maze of cliffs and chutes. When finally I reach the crest of the narrow, spinelike ridge, the place is deserted. A set of tracks leads into a snow-filled chute going down the other side. There is no doubt which way I should go. With a good look around I realize that this is the only place in sight where I could possibly get down the east slope. The route I've just come was the only way up. I search in vain for the goat. Nowhere to be seen.

Later, after dinner, I wander around the lake and its unspoiled basin. Far below, to the east, a rainbow glows over the Gallatin Range. So many rainbows I've followed these many years, and what has it gotten me? I'm not wealthy in terms of dollars, but in my own way I am a rich man. My pots of gold are these inspiring wildlands, the mountains and the deserts, the canyons and the forests. My wealth lies in the love I've gained for the simplest of flowers, the tilt of an old snag, the way the light comes through the clouds at the close of the day. Out here money is not the currency, life is.

Perched on a dry ledge of granite and gazing at the distant band of color, I hold my breath as a goat walks by within fifty feet of my still form. Another ounce of gold added to my hoard of treasure.

Wind Take Your Heart

Well, I get up with the sun and before my day is done,
I've walked a path that's all of my own.
Just like a wolverine, I'm long and I'm lean,
My heart beats with the wild wind's moan.
— from the song "Wind Take Your Heart"

I sleep much later this morning. The threatening skies of last evening dropped only a few sprinkles but prompted my use of the tent. Being inside its snug walls always adds at least an hour to my sleep time. I'm feeling like a lazy bones when I finally get up and going. But the day is perfect, and the goats are already roaming the cliffs. I climb southward, up the open basin. A goat, shaggy and losing its winter coat, appears above me nearby. The sun is behind her. A golden aura radiates like a halo around her sleek form. She stares for a moment, then vanishes.

As I skirt two small tarns, my reflection walks over their sleek, glassy surface. The air is still, the basin quiet but for the sound of murmuring water. The climb becomes steeper and I start up a snowfield, kicking my steps toward the ridge above. The sun's reflection off the snow is blinding. I close my eyes for several paces at a time, squinting my way upward.

Soon I'm cresting the narrow ridge. A goat looks up from her grazing in alarm and gallops up the slopes of Koch Peak. I follow her without my pack. The climb goes quickly. Seven goats I'd noticed earlier on the mountain are gone, but the loner I spooked from the saddle is now on the top, looking down at me with tilted head. I clamber upward, drawing ever closer. She's a curious one, leaving for a few minutes, then coming back to the edge to check my progress. When I'm nearly there she scoots away for good. A few minutes later I top out on the peak. The goat's muscular form is already nearly a quarter mile away.

From the summit I can see in one view all the ranges I plan to walk this summer: the Madison Range, the Gravelly Range, the Snowcrests, the Centennial Mountains, the Italian Peaks and the Bitterroot Range, the Pioneers, and the Tobacco Roots. The names roll off my tongue, sounding exotic and colorful. The air is clear and still. The distances seem shrunken, everything within reach. But then I turn to the east. In that direction the distances never seemed so far.

Mom is back there somewhere. Michigan might as well be another planet from this far peak. It must be about time for her morning medicine. How quickly Mom's life has changed. She was always the strong one. She had taken care of Dad during his last years in and out of hospitals. So many close calls, so many doctors and medicines, but he'd hung on for several years. It was tough on the family, but hardest on Mom. Here was her husband and partner, the breadwinner of the family, suddenly turned into the one who needed all the care. She started a business and took the reins.

When Dad died in 1980 it was as if this great burden had been lifted off Mom's back. She grieved, but then we found that she smiled easier afterwards. The temper that was often flaring during the previous years was suddenly gone. She began to travel. She loved to talk and laugh, and I think I came to know her best of all when she was living on her own, and doing so well at that.

And then this last February rolled around. She wasn't feeling good. Some doctor visits and tests, and then a diagnosis of ovarian cancer. She called me with the news, and at first it didn't register. My mom? Has *cancer*? No way. I couldn't picture her being sick. Her voice sounded so well on the phone, but she was ill and at that point had weeks of hospital time and chemotherapy ahead of her.

It's funny, looking back, I picture her doing the Twist. She'd launch into that crazy dance, shaking her big self around just to crack us up. It always did. She loves to laugh, catching up on those years that didn't hold much humor. Even now, she makes her wisecracks, trying to cheer us up. Us. She barely gets around and she's trying to make *us* feel better.

I'm looking to the east, smiling into the sun.

Back at my pack, I gaze over the deep canyon to the south. The Taylor Fork tumbles a line of churning white water through the bottom of the valley. It's a long ways down. Farther than I'd imagined. Steeper, too. Nearly 1500 feet of elevation. The talus slope is mostly dry, but here and there are big patches of snow.

I put on my gaiters (great not only for snow, but for crossing talus and keeping the rocks out of your boots) and hoist the pack. The long descent begins. Here the slope is covered with loose tiny rocks that are easy to "ski" down. I do a little jump and land on my heels. The rock begins to slide, and I let the wave of moving stone carry me down. It stops and I do another little hop, my walking stick helping me with my balance as I float down the mountain. Again and again I repeat the gliding dance. The small gravel-like rock is the easy part. It drops me smooth and fast until the stones get bigger, less moveable. Time to take a little more care or bust an ankle. Here, I must pick my way down. It's slow going until I angle over to a long snowbank and have some fun. The glissade down is quick and easy.

When the terrain flattens out a bit, I step onto firm ground, grass and solid earth. My legs wobble and feel like they're not mine, like those of a sailor fresh ashore. I turn to look back up at the ridge. Four goats, a hundred yards away, are fleeing up the frighteningly steep pitch. I'm glad I didn't see this from the bottom before I came down. It always looks so much steeper looking up.

After a short break, I hop across the Taylor Fork on a series of rocks, then begin a long climb through the forest toward a series of high basins. Here there are no signs of humankind. None of their trails or tracks. No blazes or fire rings. No sawed limbs or litter.

Instead, in the snow I cross the melted tracks of a bear, and later, the track of a lion over those of a running elk. This is true wilderness.

I wonder about that word, "wilderness." Over the centuries humankind has fought to destroy and overcome what they perceive as the threatening natural world. Even today the term "wilderness" invokes fear in many folks. It's a strange and foreign entity in the age of computers and concrete. I believe that one of the biggest threats to wild places lies in this attitude of fear. We humans tend to destroy those things that we don't understand, the things we don't know, those things that are different from what we are used to. It's too easy to be afraid. It takes no thought, no effort to attempt an understanding of things that may have no relevance in a life cut off from anything to do with the living Earth.

In a way, we Americans live a life of isolation, a life in which the Earth and the ecological systems governing it are totally absent or shut out. We're being lulled into mediocrity and pulled further away from the source of all life through the very lifestyle we've been taught to accept. Most of us don't think about how our passions for more stuff, our gasoline addictions, or our thirst for resources affects the planet that sustains us. Can we expect people who are becoming aliens on their own planet to feel anything but threatened when confronted with the Earth's untamed wonders? This fear of wildness, with all the various misconceptions and misunderstandings, can only be overcome when the word (and the world) takes on a new meaning, a new way of relating, a new ethic—one in which fear is replaced with respect, and uneasiness is overcome with trust.

This spring I talked to Ken Bacon from the *Wall Street Journal*. We were having a great conversation when he popped the question: What was my definition of "wilderness"? I'd done hundreds of interviews over the years, spoken with myriad reporters, but no one had ever asked me this simple question. My first thought spilled out, just off the top of my head. Simple, and to the point, I replied "Wilderness is a place where things work like they're supposed to work."

Later, the more I thought about it, the more I patted myself on the back. A place where things work like they're supposed to work. Yes! Of course. Where nature is allowed to run her course unimpeded and unchained. Where the living systems that have run this planet for eons are still allowed to function. Where the food chains are still intact and still working. Where flood and fire still occur. Where evolution itself is still allowed to continue. This is what wilderness is.

But can we carry this definition further? Can wilderness be a place where humans fit in, too? Where we "work like we're supposed to work?" Can it be a place where humans walk softly and are at home, traveling in harmony as a part of the place, not as a potential destroyer? A place where humans walk with respect? And is wilderness still wilderness if the great bears are gone? Or the wolves? Or the lions?

As I gain the high basins, the forest thins out. I'm among the giant whitebark pines again, both living and dead, gnarled and twisted scholars, each with a character of its own. After lunch above a small pond, I skirt the base of a sheer ridge to enter the next basin. For a quarter mile, I rock-hop across a vast boulder field. The rocks, some the size of cars, others the size of sofas, are spilled across the floor of the basin. I leap from one to another using a trick I learned long ago: Go as fast as I can. The momentum carries me into a rhythm much like a dance. No thought is involved. It's all reflex. All very Zenlike. When the rare boulder tilts to roll, I'm already on to the next. The dance is tiring but fun, and I'm soon rounding the point of the ridge and into a mountain paradise.

A clear singing stream meanders through a small bowl-like basin fringed with huge subalpine fir and scattered whitebark pine. Above the tiny basin is a moraine holding two azure blue lakes tight against the mountain's breast. Dropping the pack, I wander about, exploring the basin and deciding on the best place to camp. The wind is roaring through at regular intervals, and I try to pick a relatively sheltered spot without any dead snags hanging above the spot where I pitch my tent.

The wind is incredible. After a bath in the creek, I walk up to the lip of the basin. The Taylor Fork is a world away down below. Here the gusts come even stronger, and I stand there buffeted and blasted, letting the gale tear at my face and pull at my hair. Sometimes the air grows quiet. Dead silence with a total, numb stillness. An expectation hangs with the stillness. My ears tune in, listening and waiting. Tension builds. And then the sound comes down the mountain, races over the basin, and crashes into the trees. The wind, a living thing with a heart of its own, comes pounding toward me. I brace myself, relieved that it fills the waiting void, that once again I feel its beating embrace.

Now I curl up against a snag, comfortable with its smooth, weathered skin. This makes a good perch from which to watch the trees below waving wildly with each gust. They stand like silent herds, a part of the rock walls, until the wind comes dancing mischievously among them. Like a bear suddenly entering a calving area, the gust among the trees creates a path of wild commotion. Each tree begins to sway crazily to and fro, each limb and needle groaning and calling out, and the entire patch of forest seems ready to take up and stampede away. The path of the disturbing culprit is clearly seen. Like an invisible giant it creates footprints of singing, swaying trees. The entire range seems alive, writhing and stretching.

A lone raven comes floating by, a wind-tossed feather. Like a surfer, the raven glides and drops, soars and swoops, not fighting the wind but part of it. I'm envious, wishing I could just give myself up and let the wind carry me where it will, through the forests and over the canyons, up to the peaks and under the cliffs. To just release my "self" and let it go. To be a part of those invisible giant's footprints. To caress the wings of that happy raven. To be part of that wind. Part of the sky. I'm thinking about Mom again as the raven is carried rapidly to the east, a tiny black dot fading into the vastness of the Montana sky.

> *I see eagles a soarin', free as the wind,*
> *Maybe they're just a part of the sky.*
> *In the clouds I see faces of old mountain men,*
> *Maybe that's where they go when they die,*
> *Maybe that's where I'll go when I die.*
> *— from the song "Just a Part of the Sky"*

Back near camp, I eat dinner; the log I'm sitting on is a good thinking spot. It's one of the many downed snags—stranded mammoth trees slowly going back to the Earth. No more wind-singing for these guys. This one has been dead for many years, but up this high it'll be many more before it's finally part of the soil again. I like the feel of the dry, gray wood. Though the tree is long dead, the grain radiates a feeling of life that is soothing. I contemplate this dead tree and this wild country while I munch on a pot full of Alfredo pasta a la Stoltz.

Just when I'm thinking how likely it is that I'll be seeing bears on this trip, what looks like a bear cub comes loping across my vision, down by the creek. I freeze mid-bite. I can't see it now. Forty yards and a big tree are between us. I'm sure it's a grizz. My spoon is still poised outside my open mouth, hanging in the air. Mamma bear is going to be bounding into sight any minute now. I'm too close. Quietly, I set the pot and spoon down, eyes searching the forest. Still no bear. Now what? Silently, I do what any experienced woodsman would do—I reach for the camera.

I rise slowly, take three steps, and bend cautiously around the corner of the tree, camera to my eye at full zoom. Down by the creek, standing where I'd sat for quite some time on the big rocks, is not a bear cub but a large wolverine. She's looking directly at me and probably hears my gasp of surprise.

Already excited, now a hundred-year flood of joyful exuberance flushes through me. My voice fairly shouts, "It's a wolverine!" as she bounds off, loping distinctively up the creek and over the moraine. In seconds she's gone, as if she'd never been there. Was it just my imagination? A ghost?

I can't stop looking at the vacant ground. "A wolverine," I keep saying as I nod my head. "Wow." This is one of North America's rarest mammals. At the water's edge I look for the tracks of this legendary animal. "Wow, a wolverine." Nothing there. I gaze long and hard at the moraine, willing the rare creature to return for a longer look. But only the wind keeps coming back. I turn and walk back to my cold dinner.

My first sight this morning as I crawl from my tent is a bull elk. As startled as I am, he bolts over the hill, a thrashing retreat I can hear for several minutes. The sound travels well this morning. All is calm and quiet. The wind of yesterday has raced on to other mountains, other ravens, other lives to touch. I'm feeling in love this morning. In love with this life, this Earth, this entire universe. This wild country cloaks and warms me like a blanket. I feel secure and attuned. A cozy, content feeling fills me as I say my morning prayer, munch a quick breakfast, and pack up.

The pack feels good as I set out through the trees, then drop to round another steep ridge. The boulder field this morning is much larger than yesterday's. The rocks are sharper and seem more apt to tilt. My leaping dance sees me through, though I do have two near spills. My trusty walking stick saves me both times.

Some hikers don't like to carry a stick. I'll admit that sometimes if you're climbing it can be a hindrance. But I like a stick and rarely do I hike without one. They're nothing fancy. Just good strong pieces of dead wood. Some of them last for years and thousands of miles. Others last only a month or two. Kind of like hikers; some make it, some don't.

On my coast-to-coast trip I carried a smooth piece of driftwood from the Atlantic to the Pacific. The idea was to toss it into the western ocean at the end of the trek, but after nearly 5,000 miles of clutching that darned thing, I just couldn't do it. It had been such a trusty friend, bracing me in dozens of river crossings, propping up my heavy pack at every rest stop, letting me lean on it as I chugged my way up hundreds of mountains, and warding off more than one mean dog. I still have that stick. Always will.

This summer I'm using a piece of aspen from Colorado. It's worn smooth and polished well from the sweat of all the miles last summer. It feels right in my hand. Comfortable and strong. Doesn't mind these Montana mountains at all.

I'm in the next basin now, on firm grassy ground north of Imp Peak. But not for long. I'm aiming for a high pass on the ridge east of the peak, hoping it'll be a good route. A goat on the cliff above watches my slow approach, spying on my antlike progress for twenty minutes before vanishing into the mountain. Good enough sign for me.

I've gained the hanging valley, the only approach to the notch above. A few subalpine fir dot the narrow basin. Several brooks tumble ever downward through wide swaths of dew-covered flowers. I've been hiking for more than an hour, maybe two, and I'm still in the shade of the mountain. It's cold. The grass in the wet areas is frozen hard and crunches and crackles as I walk through.

Grizz tracks in the icy dirt at my feet are several days old but still stunning in their size and contour. My gaze sweeps slowly across the little basin. Nothing moves. Starting upward again, I realize I'm following the bear's tracks. Its use of the route is heartening. It means I've made a good choice. When I see two sets of coyote tracks going up the same way, I'm absolutely sure.

The route is steep. The snow and loose mud are slick but certainly not a problem. I'm soon stepping into the sunlight for the first time this morning. The narrow saddle is full of goat hair, and it looks like many goats have used this for a lounging spot. A long, deep drift of snow lies on the south side of the notch. I jump up onto it and look down into the basin of Alp Creek. Loads of snow still blanket this hidden valley, but trees and lakes do, too. I feel like I'm gazing down into a Wild Rockies Shangri-La. The mountains surround it like hands cradling a sacred treasure. The ridges block any views outside this alpine basin. It's an entire world all to itself.

The descent is precarious, but I pick my way down, pass a bull elk and a moose, and am soon hopping across rocks in Alp Creek. The stream here is still and deep, a product of many clear tumbling branches. I wander about the small flat, marveling at the dancing waters coming down from all directions. Each talks with a different voice. Some murmur and mumble. Others sing a constant chorus, smooth sopranos. Still others shout and even scream to the morning; a coarser, harder sound. These water voices weave together, in and out, like one unending anthem of breaks and crescendos. It's a sweet song. Perhaps there are sprites and little people in these streams. I can definitely hear voices amid the music. I look and look, as I've done dozens of times before, but I don't catch a glimpse. If they do exist, I envy them their hidden, music-filled lives.

Heading south, I climb higher into the basin, passing a series of ponds and lakes. The largest is deep and blue, with many branching arms. My topo map (1958) doesn't show it. I scratch my head and walk slowly on.

1976—Northwest Montana

I've got donuts on my mind. I want 'em bad. Big jelly-filled ones and those long, cream-filled treats. I fantasize as I walk the little dirt road. There's a town up ahead. My map shows it. I picture a little village tucked against the Kootenai River. There's got to be a little store. No donuts? Well, how about some sweet rolls? Oh, I guess I'd settle for a handful of candy bars.

I'm getting closer. It'll be nice to talk to people today. It's been a while. Gee, I should be seeing some buildings. What's that big lake doing there?

I walk closer and can see the old road disappearing into the blue waters. Disappointed and confused, I plop my pack down and dig out the map again. There's no lake here. That is, not on the old map there isn't. In front of me, and probably under a hundred feet of water, is the town. The donuts are suddenly gone. No sweet rolls or candy bars today. I've lost a few things along the way, but an entire town?

I'm staring into the water. There is no bridge. No ferry. I have no idea how long this new lake is. There will be extra miles of road walking today. Yuck! And no donuts. For some reason that upsets me more than anything. I hoist the pack and start the long walk around the new reservoir, unknown extra miles.

I'm climbing again. My second high pass today. The first part is steep. The snow is mushy, and the earth around it, muddy and slick. The wind of yesterday has returned. It threatens to push me off the mountain at every step. My balance on the steep slope is questionable as it is. Time to be careful.

When the slope becomes more gradual, I sit myself down on a high bench of the ridge that is brimmed full of wildflowers. The perch gives me a bird's eye view of this wild mountain valley I've just crossed. Four goats move slowly across the mountain a mile away. The sun feels good, and I roll back into the flowers, content to snuggle into their world.

Closed eyes allow a unique perspective of the wind. It starts way out there, far off in the depths of distance, and comes stalking. I hear and feel its approach. Lying down, I'm not much of a barrier. It roars up, tugs gently at my clothes, and races on. As it fades into the miles, I open my eyes.

The sky is cloudless. The blue is a total purity of color. The expression "bluer than blue" comes to mind. And I can lose myself in it, seeing through, and searching through, that vast space creating it, as a part of the sky, as a speck of color, as a piece of lapis, inside looking out.

My body, earthbound, lies snug against this mountain. When I close my eyes again, I search downward, into the earth, drawn into the rock beneath me by the power of the place. For a flicker of a moment the immensity of this planet lies within my grasp. The stone on stone, the billions of tons of solid rock, the miles of foundation beneath me. For a split second I can feel it all lying there against me, a part of me. Roots. For that moment I am a piece of this Earth, an atom placed just so. For that moment, I can start to understand something bigger than and beyond my tiny universe. For that split second, I can almost grasp something that feels like an answer. Eyes open, and it's gone.

After climbing again, I reach the high pass. I crouch against the wind, removing my hat so I won't lose it, and sit on the southern lip of rock, looking down the range. Echo Peak, Dutchman John, Hilgard Peak, and all their brothers and sisters stand rugged and snow covered, stretching out before me. Straight below is Sentinel Creek, where I'll meet Leslie and Derek tomorrow to resupply. I've got plenty of time.

Lunch comes and goes before I leave the windy pass and drop down a talus slope to a high camp under a huge whitebark pine. An icy brook bubbles by and the view is exceptional. The wind isn't as fierce here, and I take a bath and spend the afternoon reading and playing music. I also write a letter to my mom. This is another tradition for me. On my long treks I've always written to her, sharing the adventure, the experience, and the love of these wild places. And I know she loves to get the letters. I also know these letters on this trip will be the most important I ever send to her. I want her to know what she means to me, what these places mean to me. I want her to feel the zest of life I feel. I want her to smell the mountain flowers and feel the wind. Maybe, just maybe, the words will take her to another place. A place without cancer.

As I'm writing, there is movement at the lower edge of the meadow. A cow moose steps out from the trees and grazes uphill toward my camp. Behind her comes a fuzzy little creature, all legs and awkward. The calf is just days old and jumps about like a pup, sniffing at everything, proud of her new yet still slightly questionable mobility. They get closer, and I snap a quick picture from where I sit. Mom doesn't like the noise and realizes my presence. Her nostrils flare, and the hairs on her back (and mine) stand up. She leads the little one in the opposite direction, much to my relief, and I return to my journal.

The day slips by and the last of the wind dies to a whisper. Soon evening comes creeping over the mountains, a purple royal cloak. The full moon is rising, ripe and plump. I walk the mountainside in the eerie half light, enjoying the views of the peaks I saw today that are now decked in flaxen moonlight. Below me, the canyon is dark. Tomorrow I will be in the "civilized wilderness." I will see people and walk human trails. The mood I have experienced, the character of the land, the feelings will all be different. It'll be fun, and I'm excited for it, don't get me wrong. I do love the time with Leslie and my friends. Our most special times have been in the backcountry. But the times when I'm alone with the wilderness are those times when I feel the most connection with the wild places, the most inspiration, and the most in tune. I know I will love the time with my wife and friends, but I will be back alone soon, trekking the unvisited corners of the range, and I long for that already.

In the morning I attempt to sleep in, but feel a bit decadent in the process. After all, the world around me is wide awake, ready to go. I should be, too. Life in my little clearing is bustling. The birds are at it early, singing and squawking as soon as there's a hint of light. A few elk walk through, their footsteps a faint heartbeat of rhythm. The brook, having quieted to a murmur in the night, surges into a new tune with the coming of the sun and added snowmelt. In the comfort of my sleeping bag, I'm finally as wide awake as this new day. The sounds flow over and through me. I let them. Today I'll see Leslie. I will hear news of Mom.

When I do roll out of bed, I have a leisurely breakfast, play some music, and then take my time breaking camp. The walk down the mountain is through an ideal forest: big trees, Doug fir and whitebark pine. If I were a tree, I'd like to grow in a forest like this. Lots of room between them. Lots of space to stretch those thick limbs and sink those strong roots. Yet, with all the spaciousness, this is still a forest, a forest that I feel like I've been to before. The trees look familiar. The place feels comfortable. And I do, too.

But what's this? One moment I'm in a totally untrodden environment, the next I'm stepping onto a wide, eroded trail. The spell of the past four days is broken.

This trail happens to be the most heavily traveled in this entire designated Wilderness area. This is high, fragile country. With the snow just melting, it is still very wet and won't dry out for some time. The trail here has become a mush of muddy, braided ruts. What was once an unmarred meadow is now a mire of soupy horse tracks. I have spent a lot of time with horses. I love them. There is a long tradition of horse travel in these mountains. And many of the trails out west were originally built for packing with horses. But like a lot of things these days, we're overdoing it. Allowing such heavy equine traffic this early in the year is destroying our trails and trampling adjoining meadows as the riders skirt the mucky spots.

I turn up the trail and slop through the mud. In the space of a hundred yards I note many saw marks on the trees and two old fire rings. The contrast between this "wilderness trail" and the basins just over the ridge is startling. Is this what we've done to wilderness? Can we have high-use areas in wilderness and still call it wilderness?

I find a good sunny spot by the trail and sit myself down. The guitar comes out. I pluck it aimlessly. A few deer amble by, curious. I lean back against the pack and doze, the sound of the creek mixing with the buzz of a passing fly. I'm feeling lazy, content to lie in the sun. I'm thinking about nothing in particular, enjoying the feel of wilderness, the sounds around me, the touch of the Earth beneath me, the obnoxious whine of a distant airplane. What? My eyes pop open and I scan the skies. The noise is growing louder, more obtrusive. After only four days, I've so immersed myself in the solitude and quiet of the wild country that any foreign sound is troublesome. Isn't Wilderness (remember, capital "W" wilderness is congressionally designated) supposed to be closed to all motorized vehicles? The plane passes overhead, a blaring intrusion slicing the heart from the peace of the day. I really must write to JanSport about an idea I have for a backpacker's rocket launcher. The plane drones off into the distance. Sure sounds like a motorized vehicle to me.

If land is protected and preserved as Wilderness on the ground, why not go the whole shot? Shouldn't we have islands of quiet where Earth is allowed to live in peace? Where the wild creatures, and even humans, are allowed to experience silence? Where the ground and the skies are free of humans' stumbling, noisy passage? Shouldn't national parks, wildlife refuges, and Wilderness areas (where humans go to escape the rush and roar and press of humanity) be those rare, valued places that are free of the intrusions of humankind and are truly left to nature?

I think of all the wild places I have walked over the years, all the miles and time spent hiking in trackless country. All the days and months and even years I've spent alone in the backcountry. All that experience, yet none of it unmarred by the noise of humankind's machines. Is there nowhere to go to escape the sound of aircraft?

As part of an Arizona to Montana walk, I walked the western quarter of the Grand Canyon. For ten days the only trace of humans were the petroglyphs on the ledges I slept under. That, and the whine in the skies. The worst was a stretch of one mile when I counted thirty-two planes passing over me, some of them just a few hundred feet over the shelf of rock I walked on. It appears that we are creating our own national Disneylands by allowing so much air traffic. The noisy intrusion can't help but cheapen the experience.

My eyelids fall shut again, but I can't sleep. I know Leslie is on her way up the trail, and I'm anxious to hear about my mom. I've changed my style of walking a lot these last few years, but I've never had a resupply point so early in a trek. This is nice. I was able to start with a relatively light load, five days of food. Usually I bring ten to fourteen days' worth.

There's movement down the trail. Here comes Derek. And there's Leslie! There are few feelings as warm and as good as seeing someone you love after an absence, even one as short as a few days. Flushed with joy, I greet her. She radiates a joy shared. A hug and a kiss and here we are.

Leslie has called Michigan before hiking in. The news is good. Mom is doing better and getting stronger, even playing cards. She's moving around on her own, which is a relief. That lost mobility has depressed her most of all. To regain some of it will be a blessing. She sends me a hug that Leslie delivers with a bone-crushing squeeze.

We all sit down and gab over some lunch. I can't stop looking at Leslie. She looks good out here. Like she belongs to the mountains. She is built like a Sherpa, small but well muscled. As tiny as she is, I know she can outwalk most folks twice her size. I call her Ironwoman. With respect. She is a few years younger than I but looks even younger. I've had folks at concerts ask me if that was my daughter over there, pointing to her. She loves it! I'm not so sure if I do or not.

We share a great love for these wild places, and Leslie has spent much of her adult life working outside. For ten years she worked for the National Park Service in Yellowstone and Glacier National Parks, doing research and interpreting the mountain's wonders for visitors as a naturalist. Now she's a naturalist-guide for Lone Mountain Ranch, a private guest ranch in Big Sky. I wonder, as I gaze at her, if she knows how much I love her.

Derek says something. I'm embarrassed because I haven't been listening. He's the sous chef at the guest ranch and has brought in a big bucket of shrimp and rice stew for dinner tonight. Derek's an avid outdoorsman, at home in the woods, with an easy smile and a rugged mountain man look: shaggy brown hair and a beard.

The two of them plug me with questions. I attempt to share what I've been experiencing, all that I've seen, and just how much this wild place has touched me. The task is hopeless. I cannot express the depth of emotion. I know they don't get it. The breadth of experience cannot be crossed. How has it been? I smile. "Great," I say. "Great."

OCTOBER 1976—OLYMPIC PENINSULA, WASHINGTON

I emerge from the post office loaded with mail. Sitting next to my pack, I get comfortable and start to go through the pile. Much of it is congratulations from folks I have met along this extraordinary walk. This is the last mail stop of my coast-to-coast hike: Forks, Washington. It has taken me nearly 5,000 miles and a year and a half to get here. I'm lean and strong, proud of what I've just accomplished. Too proud.

"Hi!" I look up from the letter in my hands. A shapely, tall, attractive woman stands smiling down at me, her white teeth fairly glistening against the tan of her face. Straight blond hair falls alluringly down past her ample breasts. I catch a hint of jasmine in the air.

"Hello," I answer. Something deep down inside me is suddenly switched on. She's beautiful. She's a woman. I'm a man. Single. I tingle with interest.

"You look like a traveler," she says, nodding to the big pack.

"Yeah, I've come quite a ways." I smile modestly, waiting for her to ask where I've come from. I prepare my answer, knowing it will make a big impression. This is great.

"Where've you been?" she asks, eyes so big I could fall into them.

All right. Here it comes.

"Well, I've been walking for a year and a half now. Started on the coast of the Atlantic, up in Maine, and am bound for Cape Alava up the coast here. Just about done." I pause, waiting for the rush of amazing adoration.

"That's nice." She kind of lets the word "nice" roll out longer than it should. I feel as if my words have just passed into a vacuum. There is no comprehension at all. My words have flown over her head. Way over.

"I want to walk to Colorado some day to see John Denver," she continues. My mouth hangs open, and I stare at her as she expounds on her faith in that god of all singing gods, the Aspen troubadour. For the next ten minutes she babbles on. She has no idea what "walking" means. It's like talking to a brick. I come down fast. I deserve this. There still is justice in this world after all.

"Great," I say, "great."

Follow Your Heart

In this life that we're a-living with all its twists
*   and turns,*
It's so easy to lose our way, forget the lessons we
*   have learned,*
But the road that leads us on will always bring us
*   back,*
Once you've walked your own trail, and stepped in
*   your own tracks.*
*   — from the song "Follow Your Heart"*

I'm poking along. For some reason I'm not feeling well. Leslie and I just said our farewells again. She was the last to leave, passing over the ridge with a final call of "I love you!" The several friends that joined us for a couple nights are already on their way out. Yesterday we climbed Echo Peak.

The company has been much appreciated these past two nights, the laughs and stories a welcome hug of fellowship. It's been a break in the flow of the trip, but a fun one. Now the others are gone. I'm alone again. And I'm hurting. I'm thinking how Leslie burrows into my arms when I hug her. Of how good I sleep with her snuggled at my side. How secure that sleep can be. How in the morning, my first conscious thought is of her body lying next to mine.

Rarely do I feel lonely in the wilderness, but today I'm missing my partner. To add to my depression, my energy is totally gone. I'm feeling sick. Each step jars my kidneys. I feel nauseated. My family carries a genetic kidney disorder, and I wonder if that disorder is acting up. If I can just keep moving, maybe I can walk it through. The two miles over to Lake Ho Hand take forever.

From the peak yesterday we could see a big yellow wall tent glowing like a neon sign. I approach it now. Already depressed and grumpy, I'm disturbed by what I find. The area around the tent is trampled and torn. It looks like an army has passed through. Trees are cut, worn, and rubbed from having horses tied to them. The ground is bare, full of ruts, packed hard. This is not how folks are supposed to camp in the backcountry. It is not a respectful way to treat the wild places. I inspect the giant tent. Looks like a cook tent. Empty at the moment. It's been here a long time, some kind of permanent camp.

Permanent camps are not allowed in a designated Wilderness Area. They cause too much impact on the land. This one sure has. I've seen these camps before. In the River of No Return Wilderness of Idaho, I came across many such places, outfits that take the best campsites and hog the springs. I've even seen airstrips within the Wilderness boundaries. This all goes against the intent of the Wilderness Act, to have a place where humans are but visitors. Today, especially, it's rubbing me the wrong way.

Stepping back from the huge shelter, I fantasize over what one little match could do. Or a lightning strike. Hell, folks leave their gear up here for months, no telling what can happen to it. It's a mean thought. I'm ashamed, feeling so sour this morning. The idea of a lightning-struck tent doesn't even cheer me up. These negative musings are too much effort. I turn and walk away.

The trail is good, but I'm getting sicker. Something has affected me terribly. My bowels are rumbling and my kidneys burn. I wonder if it's the coffee I had this morning that causes this. I'm not a coffee person, not used to the foul drug. Never could see any use for it, unless it was in ice cream. Caffeine is hard on kidneys, and in the back of my mind I suspect the polycystic kidney disease is at fault for how I feel.

I try to focus on the land around me, the whitebark pines and the mountain above. It passes in a blur. I stop to defecate. In the act I notice a bear has left a monumental pile a few feet in front of me. What a relief he must have felt. I wonder what he had for breakfast. I bury three more mounds of my own in the space of a mile. I know I should stop and rest, but instinct tells me to keep moving. As I push ahead, each bend in the trail brings more pain to my kidneys and thoughts of my father's suffering from the same disease.

It's been ten years since Dad died, yet today I see him walking these trails he never walked. He's thin and bent, frail and a bit wobbly. He looks to be in his eighties. His fifties have been hard on him. Forties and thirties, too. Worked his butt off for his family and for some far-off retirement. What a deal. Dreams postponed and never realized. Pins in a map marking his son's wayward travels.

My earliest memory of "hiking"—was I even six years old—is of Dad taking all the boys, two sons and countless neighbor kids, on a camping trip. We set up the tents and then found a trail. It had a sign: "22 miles." My dad said no problem.

I wonder what he was thinking. We started off, in a line, laughing and pushing. It was hot. I don't remember any of us having water. Somewhere we got lost. Or the trail did. We beat through the fields, the marshes, the dense poison-ivy–filled forests and made it to a gravel road. It was a dry, dusty trek back to camp. I wonder how many miles we went. It seemed like a hundred to a kid. Probably only three or four, but that was a hiking trail, and we'd done it. Or part of it. And I liked it. The memory is vague, but very much there.

My dad liked the woods. He should have spent more time there. But you know work. Seemed like he was always on the run. When I was a little one, he took me with him to get new plates for the car. We parked in the shade down the block, and I remember him lifting me from the car and setting me on the ground. It was a cool spring day, the kind of day when a kid wants to run forever. I wanted to race. To my amazement, Dad obliged. My father ran down the street, a smile on his face, me chasing behind, laughing. I'd never seen my dad run. How strange. When I see him in my memories all bent and weak, I fight to envision that one morning further back, when we raced down the street.

I pass Blue Paradise Lake, trout popping from the surface like popcorn. Maybe I'm starting to feel better. I've gone more than a quarter mile without stopping. The trail begins to climb steeply. My body chugs and falters. I can't walk a step farther. Lying down in a grassy clearing, my only thought is of my dad.

Dad envied my long wanderings. By my first walk, he was too sick to come along. The huge wall map where he kept track of me was eventually covered with lines of trails I'd walked. Stick pins marked the towns I'd stopped in long enough to drop him a line. When I was with him, we spoke often of distant places. The Grand Canyon had always intrigued him. He flew over it once, long ago in a jet bound for the coast.

Dad had been dead less than a year when I first walked the Grand Canyon as part of a hike the length of Arizona. The Coconino Plateau was my approach to the Grand Canyon; three days of walking relatively flat country. I slept under a huge ponderosa pine the night before I was to reach the canyon. And though excited, I slept deeply. I'd walked eighteen miles that day. At dawn, out of that cozy sleep, I heard my father's voice, as if he were standing over me. He called to me in that familiar, sing-song lilt he'd always used to wake me when I was a child.

I bolted upright, suddenly aware. The morning was just breaking. I looked to both sides, then behind me. No one. Only the big trees towering over the empty trail.

I thought about Dad all morning as I walked northward among the ponderosa. His voice had sounded so real. As if he'd been right there with me. I came to the highway, crossed it, and walked a beeline for a mile through the trackless woods. One moment I was tramping an unending forested plain, the next I was standing at the brink of a gaping canyon, the likes of which there is no other. The space, the size, the grandeur overwhelmed me. I fell on my butt and just stared.

All day I sat there. I'd get up occasionally to walk to the edge of the cliff or wander for a short way along the rim. But I kept coming back to that first place to sit and gawk. Morning turned to afternoon and still I sat. Afternoon turned to evening. I shouldered the pack and walked along the rugged rim. A mile away I came to a small ledge, just big enough for my pack and unrolled sleeping bag. The ledge hung over the cliff like a diving board, the canyon yawning beneath it. I made myself at home.

The canyon here had a long arm that reached south for a mile or two. My perch on the west side of this gulf looked north into the heart of the canyon and east to the other wall of the side canyon. I couldn't take my eyes from the panorama before me. The sun tilted lower behind me, the shadows getting longer, the colors more alive, and the relief more pronounced.

I'd been staring into the depths of the main canyon for some time when I happened to glance over the side canyon to the smooth walls across from me. A chill crept up my spine. The shadows had formed the image of a man's head a hundred feet tall. The profile was perfect in every detail. The chin, the nose, the forehead. I knew it was perfect because I knew the man. Who wouldn't recognize their own father's silhouette? There was no doubt that Dad had made it to the canyon. And I'd like to think that he'd finally gotten to walk with me, at least for that one short day in Arizona.

An icy brook pours from the mountain where I lie. I crawl over to it, drinking as much as I can hold, and then some. The water is cold and difficult to gulp, but I've got to flush out my system, so I force myself to drink. An hour later, when I climb to my feet, I'm starting to feel better.

My steps are stronger as I climb to the next plateau. Dutchman and Hilgard Peaks, mystical castles, are floating in the clouds before me. A string of azure lakes dot the basin below. The view buoys my spirits somewhat, but I'm still missing something. I can't shake the thoughts of my family. The break with the company has disconnected me. I feel lonely. Lonely for Leslie. Lonely for my kin, some miles away, others long gone. The feelings have dragged me down.

I'm off the trail now, making my way past Painted and Cataract Lakes. The mountains' reflections shimmer only slightly in the mirror of the lakes' faces. The silence is total. I'm tempted to stop for the night at Cataract, but this strange mood has spooked me. I'm getting nervous about the off-trail route I've planned. It should be fairly straightforward, but I've grown unsure of myself. Better push on into the next basin to see how it looks.

A couple hours later, and one scary boulder field behind me, I camp on the edge of a wooded bench next to a wide rock outcropping. From atop the smooth rock I can see into the basin. The walls look steep and snow covered. They scare me. There's no way I'll get up them with a full pack. A pass directly south of me looks possible. Maybe. But it'll take me miles off my route, and there's no telling what the other side of it will be like.

I go about my camp chores, pausing every few minutes to glance up the basin at the snow and cliffs. My anxiety is building. I don't like climbing on snow.

1982—MOUNT TIMPANOGOS, UTAH

This morning atop Timpanogos comes slowly, dragging rosy hues over the peaks to the east and spilling gray across the desert to the west. It's been a long night, a cold night, with wind blasting nonstop here on the 11,750-foot summit. I haven't slept very well. The climb yesterday without an ice ax was nerve wracking. This morning I must face the descent.

Earlier this morning I was pelted by snow. The air is still cold, and I linger long in the coziness of my bag, putting off the dreaded descent for as long as I can. After a short breakfast I pack up and walk down the narrow ridge. I'm feeling better until I get to where I must drop off the east side. (I guess I shouldn't use that phrase, "drop off.") Gee, it looks steeper than it did yesterday. Maybe I should try a different route. I pull off the pack and look at the map for the ninety-seventh time. Yep, this is it. This is where I should go down. Yikes!

The map goes back in the pack. Stella (my worn, beat up, case- less guitar) is strapped down tightly on the back of the backpack. I hoist the pack up and tighten its straps, too. I grab my walking stick, give it a shake of assurance, and step hesitantly onto the ice.

Not too bad. I try another step. The snow is rock hard. I'm kicking my steps, but only getting an inch or so in. Below me the ice slides down forty yards and drops abruptly off into hundred-foot cliffs. One mistake and I could lose it all. My knees feel weak. I put my elbow out and bump the side of the hill. Too steep, but if I can just make it across to where the cliffs peter out, not even a quarter mile away, I'll be OK.

I kick a step, go a step or two, stop, catch my breath, and then try another step. It's slow. It's terrifying. It's crazy! What am I doing here? But I can't go back now; turning around on the sheer slope would be impossible. Kick. Step. Stop.

I'm trying not to look down. I'm trying to picture myself safely in the snow-filled basin below. My legs feel like rubber. I kick and step again. Not enough grip. My foot isn't holding. I'm slipping. I'm falling!

I'm sliding with my face to the mountain. I can't see the cliffs below me getting closer with every inch, but I can feel them just as clearly as can be. My feet can't catch an edge. I kick them, but the ice is too hard. My fingers claw at the sandpaper surface, skin ripping off with every inch. I'm not slowing down. In fact, I'm picking up speed, sliding steadily toward the cliffs. I'm trying to stop. Nothing's working. I'm a goner.

I roll onto my back to see what I'm going to hit when I fly off into space. The edge of the drop is ten feet below, racing toward me. I'm going to go over!

And then all is still.

I'm stopped.

I'm not dead. In fact, I'm still above the cliff. I'm dangling like a puppet from my pack straps, facing the world, the cliffs, the deadly drop into the basin. For a moment I just hang there. I'm still breathing. I'm alive. But what happened?

Hesitant to move, I tilt my head slowly, craning my neck to see but not move the pack. Stella! My guitar! The old beater is lashed snugly onto the back of my pack without a case, with the neck pointed down. The neck of the guitar has gouged deeply into the icy crust, sticking like an ice ax and lodging me firmly to the ice field in a spot barely feet above the edge of the drop off. Soaked with sweat, and with pounding heart, I sigh and settle back. I need to think about this.

Hiking on steep snow makes me nervous. Each time I look up the basin I feel a bit more on edge. I know that when I get closer and get up on the face of the wall, it won't be as bad as it looks from here. And going up is always easier than coming down. But I can't shake this anxiety. Combined with my already dour mood, I've lost the comforting effect wild country always holds for me. My negative feelings are blinding me to the surrounding beauty. Instead of soothing me, the wonderland has become a threatening prison, and I'm not entirely aware of how high I've hoisted those dark walls.

It looks like it may rain, so I set up my tent. (Five drops is all I get. I know because I count them.) Before starting dinner I find a good tree to hang my food from. No bear is going to get the cookies Leslie made for me. I uncoil my rope, tie a rock around one end, and toss it expertly over the limb I've picked out, high above me. The rope comes floating back down in my face as the rock, coming untied, flies into oblivion. Let me try this again.

I find another rock, tie the rope, and toss it again. It misses the damn limb. Not only that but the rock comes loose again. #@^&@#*!

I search for another rock. It seems I've thrown them all. In the mountains of Montana, I can't find a bloody rock! A guy could get a mite disturbed doing this.

When I do find another one, it's a bit too small, but I think it'll do. I tie it up good and tight. This one will never come off. I take a deep breath. Relax. My throw is right on. The rock arcs beautifully over the limb. And stops.

Now, the idea behind this method is that the rock will carry the end of the rope back down to where the hiker stands waiting. I'm waiting. The darn rock is too light. I try to jiggle it, give it some slack, but it just hangs there like a balloon. @#^&#**@&#*!

OK. I'll bring it back down, find another rock, and start over again. I pull on the rope, the rock promptly becomes wedged in the forks of the branches. I pull, thinking the rock will come loose from the rope, but no, I had to tie it so it would never come off.

Maybe I can pull hard enough to break off the little limb it's stuck on. I tug away for several minutes, achieving nothing except rope burns on my hands. The air is blue by now. I'm inventing new curses by the minute. This isn't going to work.

I search out a fallen limb and find one that's nearly twenty feet long. I can barely lift it, but I manage to carry it over to my stuck rope with hopes of using it to dislodge the rock. Muscles straining, I hold it up. It teeters wildly like a drowsy monster searching for its prey. When it finally finds the rock I push with all my strength. A limb breaks and my pole flies dangerously astray. I duck and dodge as it comes pounding back to earth. My rope and rock are still hanging.

Ah, the peace of the mountains. I'm afraid I'm not a kind visitor to the basin this evening. Curses do not describe the words I utter. I pull on the rope, thinking maybe I can break it. I try climbing the tree. I throw other rocks at it. I've been at it for nearly an hour. Then the best thing: I turn my back on the tree, go over to the ledge of rock, and sit down.

I can't help but look up at the head of the basin. The walls of rock and snow rise like an impenetrable barrier. A dark cloud hangs over the basin, and my camp feels gray and oppressive. The day has not been easy on me. Nor have the last months. My throat tightens. I greatly miss my dad. I'm so worried about Mom. A tear creeps out the corner of one eye. Another one follows it. In a rush, they are joined by a torrent. I can't remember the last time I had a full out, get-down sob session. It feels good to let the tears wash down my cheeks. I cry out fear, frustration, pain, loneliness. I cry for my mother, my father, the wilderness, the planet, and me. It spills out. The release is total, a flood of emotion built up over the past months sweeping through my heart.

I'm still sitting there with my tear-stained face when a beam of sunlight finds its way through the layer of clouds. The light pours through the gray sky, flashes across the dark rock of the mountains, and radiates like a living thing. It shines down like a curtain of glory, a heaven-sent pat of assurance, a magnificent ray of hope pouring into the basin. I've witnessed these displays of light before, many times, but never have they touched me so deeply and so thoroughly. It's as if this sudden shaft of light has allowed me to see myself. I've been sad, scared, and hurt, and I haven't handled it well. I've just kept taking it in and taking it in and burying it deep inside. It has shut me off from the things I seek here, but now it has shown me something else. Wilderness has reminded me of my own humanity. It has stripped me down and made me look at my own frailties. By showing me my weaknesses it has strengthened me. In that moment of realization, I'm released from the prison of doubt I've locked myself in. I feel like a new person. I look up the basin and shrug. I know I'll find a way. There's always a way.

I turn back to the tree. In five minutes I have the rock down and my food rope hanging in place. Things are looking up.

A hard wind last night has cleared and polished the morning to a buffed shine. I'm feeling new and fresh. How could I have felt so down last night? Instead of apprehensive, I'm excited. Breaking camp takes too long.

The south fork of Hilgard Creek flows wild and strong. I jump across on big rocks and climb a snowy hill. A little lake, not shown on my map, greets me over the rise. One side is walled by a moraine of rocks and boulders; the other is cloaked with big trees. A dipper dances steadily in the shallow outlet pool, bobbing and fluttering in the first rays of the day, which glisten on the mirrorlike surface of the water. The scene is flawless; I feel that a hurried step might crack the picture. Soft steps, slow thoughtful ones, are much more appropriate here. A slow step gives time, adding to my day, adding to my store of thought and memory. It allows the sights and smells to soak deeper into my wayward being. It allows me to be here longer.

Beyond the lake, the trees thin out and disappear. I follow two sets of coyote tracks into a world of ice and rock. The air is still and as solid as the frozen earth I walk over. The coyotes' trails turn back. I wish I could look down on myself from the heavens right now. I'd be a tiny speck of movement in this immense, still, silent world. It would be hard to tell I'm even moving. I'd be hard to see, an ant crossing the mountain's spine.

The headwall I will ascend is getting closer now, and it's looking much friendlier, just as I knew it would. I leave the basin floor and start up a slope of talus that becomes ever steeper as I gain the snow. I kick each step deeply and firmly. Securely. The morning fills me with respect and exhilaration. In a way, I'm using that to power me up, through each foothold, past each grasping handhold. In no time I'm topping out on the narrow ridge, soaked with sweat and huffing like a spouting whale. I look back down the way I've come. Not too bad.

A comfortable nook in the boulders atop the ridge takes me in. I like how the big rocks cradle me. Nice and solid, they are already warming to the new day. From my perch I can study the basin below me, to the south. Avalanche Lake sparkles in the sun. Studded about it, in the rocks and scattered forest, are a dozen other azure ponds. I gaze out over the scene for minute upon minute, mesmerized by the fresh newness of the place. Paradise must look something like this. Perhaps in paradise, it's always morning.

The shrill squeak of a pika breaks through my reverie. That little squirt! Where is he? I scan the scattered rocks about me. Nothing moves. The squeak comes again, closer now. I still can't see him. Wait. A slight movement off to my left gives him away.

The pika, sometimes known as a rock rabbit, is a small member of the rabbit family. It is much smaller than a rabbit, about half the size of a guinea pig, without a tail, and sporting a set of short, rounded ears. The gray color and rounded shape of the pika enables it to blend in with the rocks. The camouflage protects the pika from predators such as eagles, foxes, martins, and occasional hungry hikers. Just kidding on that last one.

I saw my first pika on Scapegoat Mountain years ago and became an instant fan of these rugged little creatures who have the bark of a child's squeak toy. They live year-round where I'd like to, the high alpine areas of the western mountains. All summer long and into the fall you can find them busy gathering their winter's supply of food, making hay, collecting grasses, and stockpiling little mounds of it hidden in the rocks. Often I've come upon a little pika dragging a four-foot piece of pika groceries steadily up a steep mountain. Their energy is endless. They refuse to hibernate when the snows come. Instead they build tunnels to their various widespread hay caches and dream of spring when they can get back to work.

⌒

I walk the ridge; moss campion and phlox dot the rocks. Six mountain goats are grazing peacefully a quarter mile away. This is my last day in the Madison Range. I walk slowly.

The peak I climb doesn't have a name, at least not on my map. It doesn't really need a name. Not enough people go there to climb it. Names are only for people. The ravens that soar on the mountain's air currents don't have a name for it. Nor do the goats that roam its slopes. The clark's nutcrackers who flock there by the dozen have no use for nomenclature. If they did, they'd probably call it "the shitting place." That's what they do, stopping on the rocks as they fly from one side of the range to the other. Stopping to drop a load. Perhaps it helps their flight down the other side.

So much bird guano covers this peak that I have trouble finding a clear place to sit. I turn a rock over and perch on it. The day is clear, and I wonder how many hundreds of square miles are within my sight at any one moment. The Gravelly Range across the valley to the west is where I'm heading. It looks smooth and soft, not nearly as wild as where I now sit. We'll see.

North of me is Hilgard Peak and the bulk of the Madison Range. I've only been out a bit over a week, but I feel as if I've made more progress than any week could give. The wilderness has touched me where it always does, in the heart. It has stirred emotions and feelings that relate not only to the land, but to every aspect of my life. That strange hybrid of thought and mood has begun to sprout into a life of its own. The wild country is a seed, the closeness and accessibility of passion one of its tastiest fruits.

Wilderness Walks Within

Yes, I'm holding the memories of moments,
Of the times and the places that I've been,
It rides in my soul and I won't let it go,
Remembering the sweet summer wind.
     — from the song "Wilderness Walks Within"

The morning brings the din of a hundred birds. My eyes pop open and scan the branches of the old Doug fir towering over me. The ancient wrinkles in the tree's bark are comforting. I feel secure here, as if my closeness to something so old and alive passes some of that life on to me. I've slept well under the big tree. The moon, big and bright, bathed even this forested canyon in a soft, silvery light. It's good to sleep under such a moon. It's enchanting, bewitching, even. The world is painted with a different perspective on such nights, and those who are out in it see the same sights, but from a unique angle. How can life help but be enriched by

58

such a viewing? I definitely feel wealthy this morning, lying in my bag, hands propped behind my head, grinning at the morning, happy from my heart to my head to my soul. Papoose Creek is a distant murmur a hundred yards away. A doe wanders by on the other side of the tree. I suppose I should get up, but this bag is so comfortable.

An hour later I'm walking a jeep trail, dropping lower and lower into the valley and closer to the Madison River. The forest has given way to rolling meadows carpeted with lupine, balsam root, and sticky geranium. Dew sparkles on each pedal and leaf. The first rays of the sun are warming the fields, stirring the sweet aroma of the flowers with that of the moist grass and damp earth.

A few miles bring me out to a trailhead, and a short ways farther I come down to a paved highway. Here I am suddenly an alien, an eagle in a cage, a bear walking through a mall. I walk the shoulder for a quarter mile. In that time I see five cars, three dead birds, one flattened garter snake, two beer cans, and eleven No Trespassing signs. Welcome to civilization.

The absurd pettiness of my own kind puts wings on my feet. I walk fast to get off the ribbon of pavement, to leave this squashed world behind. The turn off the highway leads me immediately to a bridge over the Madison River. This main tributary of the mighty Missouri has its headwaters in the heart of Yellowstone. Here, between the Madison and Gravelly Ranges, the waters are still clear. They haven't been polluted by the insecticides, the pesticides, and the dozens of other "cides" that will foul the river on its way to the gulf. The Madison doesn't have the murky look of the Missouri. It has its youth, a fresh vitality, a strength of truth, a blind promise that it can never live up to. The river looks blue, like a kid's drawing colored in. I cross it on a one-lane steel bridge, stopping to gaze down into the pure, silken waters flowing steadily on and on. How nice it would be to float down those rolling waters. The river pulls my thoughts in, holding me, taking me back to a hundred rivers far down my long trail.

OCTOBER 1985—BETSIE RIVER, MICHIGAN

My brother, Mark, is a big guy. He's my height, 6'3", but stout and strong. Reminds me of black bear with his full dark beard and roly-poly build. He's three years older than me, and like any little brother, I suffered greatly when we were kids. Seems like I was always getting talked into doing dumb things under his advisement. It's funny how maturity can turn things around.

We try to do things when I'm in Michigan. That's where he lives, where I used to live. This year we've planned a three-day canoe trip down the Betsie River. We've paddled a lot together. I'm in much better control than he is. Of course, he thinks just the opposite. We go round and round about it. Mark says I learned to paddle by reading a book. He always gives a little scoffing laugh as he says it. I laugh, too, because I did!

We've beaten our way across a big lake, wind fighting us the entire way. I'm in the stern, in control, but he got us across. Without his brawn we'd still be out there. We're glad to be in the current again as the river leaves the lake. It sweeps us easily along.

A bridge appears ahead. It's a low bridge, a very low bridge, hanging mere feet above the flowing waters. A spot on the bank looks like a good place to pull out. It'd be a quick, easy portage, but I think we can make it under the bridge. In fact, I know we can.

Mark points over to the shore, very sure of himself. I keep the canoe headed for the bridge.

Mark says, "Better pull her over."

I keep it headed downstream.

Mark yells, "Pull over! What ya doin'?"

"I think we can make it," I offer as I keep drifting toward the bridge.

Mark is getting excited, yelling at me to turn it. I'm starting to laugh, keeping the canoe headed right for the bridge. Mark is really excited now. He's waving to the side, swearing and shouting. I'm shouting now, too.

"Duck, Mark, duck! We can make it!" I whoop with glee.

"Pull her over." He's trying to draw to the side.

"No, let it go straight! Duck!" I'm countering Mark's strokes bringing the canoe back toward the low gap I'm hoping we'll fit through.

Mark has grabbed the bridge. The canoe starts to turn broadside to the current, the river piling up against it. Looks dangerous. Water threatens to spill in and swamp us. Mark hasn't stopped yelling for a second. "You trying to kill us or what?"

I'm laughing even wilder now, shouting to let her go. Duck! Mark ducks, laying his big form back against the packs behind him, and barely scraping under the bridge. Curses echo as if from a faraway canyon, reverberating like waves across the flowing river. And then I'm forced to

*lie back myself, flat over the tail of the canoe, pushing up on the bridge
to force the canoe lower. My chest scrapes the weathered beams, mud,
birdshit, and spiderwebs falling in my face. Mark's voice is a steady
metallic ringing of profanity. I can't breathe. I'm hysterical. Tears mix
with the dirt falling on my face, and my open mouth collects wayward
debris. I'm barely making it, just squeezing through, and wondering
about my large brother.*

*We pop out the other side, like a submerged cork breaking the sur-
face. Mark is laughing now, but still yelling just to give me shit. I'm
howling. We're covered with dirt and river splouge. Finally I manage to
gasp, "Hey, I knew we could make it."*

After leaving the river, I begin climbing. The trail shown on my
national forest map isn't marked on the ground, and I don't have the
topo maps for this stretch. After searching for the trailhead unsuc-
cessfully for some time, I head up the mountain in the direction I
think the trail should go. The going is steep and difficult, with many
downed trees, but I'm glad to get away from the road again, and after
a half mile I find old blazes and the overgrown trail.

It's hot now. Even in the forest the big firs smell as if they're being
kiln-dried, the sweet scent of pitch overpowering the hillside. I'm
sweating buckets. My T-shirt is soaked, sticking to me like a layer of
skin. It feels good to sweat, good to work. This first week has whipped
me into shape. Feels like I've never been away from it. Each step, each
huff of air, each drop of sweat is a blessing today.

I can't help but think of Mom. If only I could share some of this
strength I feel. I wonder how she'd feel if she could sit in these mountains for an hour. I wonder what being atop a Montana mountain
could do for someone so ill as she. Dad always expressed a desire for,
and an envy of, my travels in the wild country. But, I wonder about
Mom. It's funny that I never asked her if she ever longed for the big
trees or the wide, sweeping spaces , or the snowy, shining mountains.
I wonder if she ever just wanted to leave it all behind and head out. I
must remember to ask next time I talk to her.

The sound of the highway nags me for at least two miles, creeping
across the distance and flitting through the forest as if it were stalking
me. It steals my serenity each time I pause in search of quiet. At last
the sound is swallowed by the still, silent trees I find myself walking

among. The only sound is the creak of my pack, my rhythmic breathing, and the fall of one boot following another. I seem to be a highway of noise myself. If only I could swoop as silent and as smooth as the gray jay.

A few miles from the river I top out on a high bench that's been clear-cut and is a maze of forest roads. I'm aiming for Standard Creek, looking for the trail leading down to it shown on my big map, but with the tangle of old roads through the ugly cuts, I'm totally confused. I don't like this. Not one bit. Better to bushwhack down to the creek and just follow it upstream. I should hit the old trail somewhere along the way.

One minute I'm beat by the sun in a clear-cut, the stumps piled haphazardly amid the scrawny new growth, and the next, I'm stepping through a time machine, walking under a shady canopy of big healthy firs and spruce. Once in their shelter I breathe easier, realizing just how tense I was walking through the cut. These places always hold a mood of violence, hanging like a cloud even on the clearest day.

I keep going northward as I begin to drop toward the creek far below. Without a path, the going is slow, but I'm in no hurry. The forest is beautiful, with several tiny glades and mossy springs tucked among the trees. The silence is total but for my clumsy tramping and breathing.

The slope gets steeper and the trees get closer together. I walk carefully here, climbing over and around blowdowns, trying to keep my footing. The stream is closer. Its roar gets louder with each foot I descend.

The last fifty feet are the toughest. I plunge through briars and fall over a mossy log into a mucky pit, struggle through a patch of stinging nettles, and at last come to stand next to the gurgling creek. I'm surprised by its size. Up above it sounded like a mighty river. Here it is a pleasant little creek, six or eight feet across. The water is cold and clear. I lap it up and splash it over my face, dipping my cap and soaking it. It'll cool me as it dries.

The trail should be around here somewhere. I jump the creek on a log and slog up the steep slope on the other side. Nothing. Hmmm. As long as I keep along the creek, I should merge with it eventually. This north side is steep and full of blowdowns. I angle back down and cross back to the south side. Blowdowns here, too.

The forest along the creek is beautiful but unforgiving. The going is slow. Hard work. Nettles and thorns scratch at my legs as I jump over and around the downed trees and back and forth across the little creek. I'm soon covered with scratches and streaks of blood. If I pause for but a moment, a cloud of mosquitoes envelops me. Must keep moving. I fall again. Pieces of my skin adorn more than one stub of a broken branch. I wonder how long I can keep this up.

AUGUST 1987—NORTHERN SWAN RANGE, MONTANA

The mountain before me is a thick wall of green. Gripping the nearest bush, I pull my body upward, the limbs pulling and scratching, fighting every inch of progress. I have to rest again, holding on to the shrubs to keep from falling back. Huckleberries, hundreds of them, plump and ripe, dangle in my face. Without releasing my handholds, I can tilt my head and pluck the sweet berries into my mouth with my tongue.

Behind me I hear the others. I turn to see how they're doing. Two faces floating in the tangle of leaves grin up at me. Below them is the top of someone's pack. Two others are totally invisible in this Montana jungle. Their nearby voices are the only trace of their presence. We've entered the twilight zone of backpacking.

Three hours ago, in a huge clear-cut, we lost the trail, but there's another trail only a mile away. An easy hike to the crest of the ridge. Only a mile

Only? And I'm the leader? Some leader. "Follow me!" . . . "Grab onto this bush here!" . . . "Watch that log there!" . . . "You can't see it. Use your feet to feel it." . . . "It's got to thin out soon." . . . "Have a huckleberry."

We fight our way through the brush, a foot at a time, pulling ourselves up and through the dense barrier of growth. The others get tired of hearing me whoop with joy at all the berries. They weary of my "we're almost there" comments. It gets to be a joke. A couple get strangely silent. But we keep at it.

At last we stagger out onto the packed trail. Our arms, legs, and faces are covered with a curious combination of stains. The red of our blood is mixed with the purple of the huckleberries, the green of the leaves, and the brown of the good earth. That solitary mile has taken us five and a half hours.

Later, I find the trail. It leads into a beautiful stretch of the canyon. The creek here is smaller and cascades among the feet of the craggy old fir trees. The trail makes walking easy, and I revel in the sights of the big trees, the rushing, cool waters, and the mossy rocks.

A few miles up, I find a series of funny orange streamers. Some people call it survey tape. They glow from their perches atop little stakes dotting the creekside, ranging up the mountain's slope. Someone had a party and forgot to pick up after themselves. Thoughts of Ed Abbey come to my mind as I sigh, take off my pack, and begin to pick up the unsightly litter. It takes only ten minutes and the armload of trash is easily buried. The forest is silent and waiting when I start on. It stands intact today, but I wonder: How long will these trees shade the silent canyon?

The trail joins a rustic lane, and the canyon broadens into a wide valley. The stream here is braided, winding and slow. It slips through a maze of willows, veins of silver lacing a wide, green plain. Looks like good moose country.

It's time to make camp, but immediately upon stopping, I'm attacked by a hoard of mosquitoes. I consider hiking on, but I'm tired. Seventeen miles today. I guess I'll just have to put up with the extra company. The air is alive as the tent goes up, abuzz with the pesky drone. Bare arms, legs, and neck are prime targets until I slip on long pants and a hooded raincoat for protection.

Once my camp is set up, it's time for my number-one priority. Dreams of a bath have walked with me all day. The blood, sweat, and grime have to go. I climb down the bank into the creek bottom. The din of the mosquitoes takes an upward turn. There's a break in the streamside foliage where I can get close to the water. The creek is only five feet wide here, but in the bend is a pool at least three feet deep. Looks good to me.

Off come the boots, then the socks. Bare feet are suddenly transformed into mosquito prime rib. I'd better be quick about this. I'm tearing off my clothes like a madman. As each new square inch of skin is exposed, it is covered with a dense layer of hungry mosquitoes. The removal of each garment is a dinner bell to a hundred more blood-craving bugs. I spit and curse as my limbs tangle in the rush to get it over with.

At last I'm standing naked, swatting wildly about me. I take another swipe and jump for the pool. Yikes! That's cold! I pause in mid crouch, but then slowly lower myself, welcoming the water's icy touch, savoring the smooth caress enveloping every inch of my dirty, tired body. Like an alligator, I float with just my eyes and snout above the water. When the bugs discover me, I dip down, laughing under the surface. This is heaven.

Scrubbing off the day's collection of blood and dirt, I begin to feel the cold invading my bones. I've been in here for ten minutes. I don't want to get out. I know they're waiting for me. Out there. I can hear them. I know they're going to swarm all over me. I'll have to dry off before dressing again, and then there's my dirty shirt and socks to rinse out, too. But there's a chance, maybe with all this dirt and stink removed, that the bugs won't recognize me.

I jump up and step onto the bank. The mosquitoes don't recognize me. No, instead they think they've found something even tastier. In moments I'm covered again.

~

It's cold. Frost coats the meadows. Thinking of the hoards of bugs that will rise here when the day warms, I have no trouble getting an early start. I walk the jeep road, stepping fast to keep the chill off. The pace feels good, the rhythm my only thought. Muscles chug away. Lungs pump like bellows. It's a smooth, endless tread.

The landscape becomes more pastoral as I ascend, with more meadows and wider vistas. Two elk, young bulls, eye me warily and trot over a knoll. A red-tailed hawk screams overhead, its tail flashing crimson in the morning sun. On the crest of the range I meet a gravel road. For two easy miles I walk it north before turning once again to a faint trail and into more roadless country. The track leads me higher. Expansive views of the Snowcrest Range open to the west. Its mountains look soft and green, inviting from here. I'll be walking the ridge there in a few days.

The trail leads me over flower-cloaked slopes and into Tepee Basin. Deer graze along the creek, and marmots whistle from the hillsides. A coyote barks at me and lopes smoothly away. Over another couple ridges in the mud next to upper Ruby Creek are several fresh black bear tracks. I'm so pleased to find such havens of wildness that I'm stopping often just to gaze out across the open slopes, savoring the scent of rough, untrodden land.

In late afternoon I come out into one of the most beautiful, most expansive mountain meadows I've ever come across. The flowers extend as far as I can see. It's as if a rainbow has somehow fallen to the Earth, shattering into a million tiny fragments. Each color is well represented, splashed to the horizon over the vast meadow. Across the wide Madison Valley, the Madison Range rises clear as can be. The Sphinx, rising sharply above the valley, looks almost touchable, massive and imposing.

The trail is like a ball and chain here, shackles holding me back. I can't help but leave it to wander about the mile-wide field, oblivious to where I'm going, intent only on the flowers at my feet, the spacious view I am a part of, and the barrage of scents I am now bombarded with. The sweet scent of lupine, the punky, dirty-sock smell of bistort, and the rich summery geranium flood together in a heady perfume enveloping the slope. The meadow itself seems hung in the sky, suspended over the valley and the day. I hang suspended with it for some unmeasurable time, enchanted by this bouquet of color I've stumbled upon. The meadow releases me, returns me to my senses, only when I reach the edge of the forest.

It is like coming out of a dream. I shake my head and look about me. No trail. Which way should I go? As I reach for my map, a great horned owl launches itself from the limbs of a gnarled fir. He floats eastward through the open forest. No need for maps now. I follow it east—down, down, down.

Listen to
the Earth

Have you ever heard the mountains move when
  the rocks come tumblin' down?
It seems the world is going to end, but it's just
  shifting itself around.
It happens all the time, my friend, it's all been
  done before,
There's something there, I know there is,
If we listen to the Earth once more.
                    —from the song "Listen to the Earth"

The Snowcrest Mountains are one of Montana's best-kept secrets. Most folks have never heard of them. Mention them to the average Joe or Josephine and the usual response is, "The what mountains? Huh?"

The name has a nice ring to it. Snowcrest sounds pretty, and wild, too. And it should. One of the largest elk herds in the state roams there. Occasional grizz, too. It's just a tiny range, but on the map it has that dark brown color signifying no motorized vehicles. I have to go there.

Now, a day after leaving the Gravelly Range, I'm switchbacking up Snowcrest Mountain on an overgrown trail. The grade is quite gradual. The hike isn't difficult. I'm glad after yesterday's twenty-four miles.

Looking back across the Ruby Valley, the Gravelly Range looks nondescript from here, the mountains round and tame. I know now that the land there is laced with roads and clear-cuts. In many cases the land has been ill treated and overgrazed, but tucked away among those rolling ridges are some fairly large stands of wild country. These remnant wildlands hold hope for the survival of the range's very core. What's that line from Aldo Leopold? "The secret to intelligent tinkering is to save all the pieces." Those last pockets of roadless land are the pieces we must be sure to save, especially if we ever decide to try to put things back together. Leopold was a man who saw things clearly and had a great way of expressing environmental truths. He once wrote, "A man is rich in proportion to the number of things he can afford to leave alone." I can't help but wonder how rich we will allow ourselves to become.

The switchbacks are endless, or seem to be. But I'm enjoying the endless rhythm I find myself a part of. It's a rhythm of movement, a constant working of bone and brawn. For a while it's as if I'm walking on a treadmill, pounding away, but getting nowhere. I feel suspended in time and place.

Mom must be up and about by now. Probably sitting in her big chair in the living room. Maybe holding her new granddaughter, Jessica. Smiling. The new life brightens the world. The old gives to the new, and then gives way for it. Again and again. Ebbing and flowing.

Cancer has become so commonplace in our society. Cancer of this, cancer of that. And we have largely accepted it as a way of life, not out of the ordinary in any manner. Much as we've accepted the crowding and polluting of our planet. While we may not be in total denial, we still have not realized that this is not the way things are supposed to be.

A world in balance is not one in which one species dominates. An Earth living in harmony is not one in which water and air are constantly polluted, where every last corner of the Earth has been affected by the hand of humankind. Cancer is often a direct result of an unhealthy environment. It is not something we have to live with. Clean up the planet, and we clean up our health. Why is this lesson so hard to learn?

My mother proudly displays a "Listen To The Earth" bumper sticker on her car. I gave it to her. It could say "Listen To Your Mother." Somewhere along the line we have gained an arrogance that has plugged our ears. When I was young, if Mom told me to do something and I ignored her, I could expect a whipping. What will we get from ignoring the appeals of Mother Earth?

The crest of the broad ridge is covered with a wide array of flowers. Lupine are everywhere. The aroma is intoxicating. Fifty elk graze on a shoulder of the ridge below me. They scatter and vanish as I walk the open mountainside. One moment they're there, the next they're gone.

I'm walking much slower today. Yesterday I felt like Mr. Machine. A lazy feeling rides on the scent of the flowers. Like Dorothy in the Wizard of Oz, I keep sitting down in the field of lupine. It's another clear day, and I can see for hundreds of square miles. Those miles are too much for me today. They weigh like bags of sand, heavy on my backpack, and it all seems so far.

The ridge leads me southward, paralleling the Ruby River and the Gravelly Range to the east. Walking the spine of the mountain is like walking a bridge through the heavens. My track leads through the skies of Montana. The ravens call to me. The cry is familiar and comforting. The rock and flowers at my feet are a path in themselves. They lead. I follow. The mountain itself has become The Way.

The trail had disappeared when I first topped out on the ridge. Now the open crest leads me above a branch of Cream Creek. Here it's as if a massive bite has been taken from the Earth. The mountain has broken off and slid toward the valley. Jagged cliffs break upon piles of rock debris spilling down the canyon. It all looks so recent, so fresh. I perch on the rim, wide-eyed, expecting the river of rock to start moving again any moment. I scan the waves of piled stone, waiting. It never happens. Perhaps another 10,000 years or so. You never know.

Footsteps
(Spring of 1988—Grand Canyon, AZ)

Moving rock,
Like falling trees,
Decides on its own when to go,
Whether or not a body's there to listen,
To watch the dust rise after,
Ponder that split second of Time.

Then, is it time to count your stars
To add another wonder,
Piling up grains of sand,
And uncountable pages to leaf.

In the shade of the overhang
We sought shelter from the rushing storm.
Our world grew dark and silent,
But for the rain.
We huddled in our sleeping bags
Listening to kisses,
Water to rock, rock to water,
Gentle lovers touching just so.

The thunder came at night,
Blazing flashes of sight and sound
Crashing to the cliffs,
Sinking into each pore of every rock
And ourselves.

We made love in our cave.
Wild, with the storm,
Loud in our heated bodies.
In my arms, afterward,
Her heart beat like thunder

Into mine
With the power of the lightning.

Listening,
We lay with the rock.
Waiting
For the next crack through the sky.

It came then,
A bit of thunder hidden in stone.
Paused for an eon's breath,
Waiting only for the screaming rain,
The mountain moved.
A pondering giant shook its shoulders.
The sleeping rock awakened.

Below, we felt it roll,
Our bones trembling with the earth.
Pounding steps, end over end,
It raised thunder on its own,
Coming closer,
And bounced into the abyss,
Carried away,
Like fallen seconds lost to eternity.

Still no signs of any trail here, but I leave the ridge and descend into the upper basin of Spring Creek. The trees grow in little groves separated by rolling meadows and steep gulches. In one patch of forest I come upon an old hunting camp. In the shade of the big Douglas firs, a spring gushes from the ground, arctic cold, bubbling over rocks coated with neon green moss. All about are white columbine. A rusty tin cup hangs from a nearby tree. When I drink from it, the flakes of iron add an odd, tinny spice to the water. It tastes old.

After lunch I spend the afternoon skirting the western slopes of the range, heading generally southward. The grassy slopes and scattered timber make the travel easy, and I pause several times to sit and watch a pair of golden eagles playing in the air currents overhead. I also keep a close watch on my map. For several miles there are no trails, and I try to keep myself oriented to exactly where I am.

Maps have a certain romance to them. Each name conjures up a dozen images, and a hundred questions. I can spend hours day-dreaming over maps, searching out routes this way, and exploring possible paths that way. I love the ring of certain names. You can tell a lot about a place just by the handles tagged on it. Sometimes.

This particular U.S. Forest Service (USFS) map I'm using is a great one for armchair travelers. It covers all the USFS and BLM lands in southwest Montana. Last night I spent quite a bit of time gazing at the map. The Snowcrest Range itself is full of imagery: Sawtooth Mountain, Yellow Bear Lake, Sunset Peak, Stonehouse Mountain, Honeymoon Park—now there's a name to conjure up some images. And look at all the critter names. Wolverine Creek, Crow Creek, Deer Creek, Blacktail Deer Creek, Bull Creek, Badger Creek, Fawn Creek, Dog Creek, and Bear Creek. The place gains some character just from its nomenclature.

Yes, the unknown heroes who named these places sure had inspiration to work with, but what happened when they came up with No Name Creek? Must have had a bad day. Or maybe they figured all the best names had been taken. I suppose it's a much better name than a boring one like Rock Creek. There are six Rock Creeks on this one map. In fact, as I think about it, there are many overused names on this map: five Bear Gulches, four Bear Creeks, five Sheep Creeks, three Sheep Mountains, three Table Mountains, four Beaver Creeks, four Cottonwood Creeks, four Mill Creeks, and the most used title of all: seven Dry Creeks. So much for creativity.

One name that I've been curious about is Devil's Hole (only two of them on the map). The places sound rugged and wild, forbidding and hard to travel in. The kind of places where I'd like to camp. When finally I get to one of them, I'm a little disappointed. Oh, the little valley is indeed beautiful, but it doesn't look like it sounds. It seems softer, more inviting. Nice big trees and flowers splashed everywhere. Not the kind of place a devil would like to hole up in. The wash in the canyon is dry, but the earth is damp. The grass and flowers are lush. I wade through the deep growth, breaking green waves at my knees. The air is still. The only sound is the cry of a gray jay, the swish of my passing.

I stop to take a break and set the pack down on a bare patch of ground. Woah! Wait a minute. At my feet in the soft mud, a bear track lies neat and tidy. It's like a picture perfectly placed, hung just right, every detail etched in clear acrylic. It's big. Damn big. And fresh, too.

I glance over my shoulder and around the canyon, scratching my head. I can't believe what I'm seeing. Looks like a grizz track. The claws stick out far ahead of the pads. Big claws. I know the Snowcrests see an occasional passing grizzly bear, but I never thought I'd see any sign of one. Grizzly bears could get here easily enough, but once here, it'd be as if they'd fallen into a black hole. The cattle industry sees to that by killing any big predators that share the mountains with their cows. A bear here would have to be pretty smart to keep out of the way of people. It'd have to keep a pretty low profile. Maybe hang out in a place like Devil's Hole.

I scan the hillsides around me, long and slow. The fact that a grizzly bear has been here is good to know. The place feels better to me. A touch wilder. A bit farther back. A little more precious. Hell, how many places on this Earth feel the tread of the grizz anymore? I think I'll walk just a little farther before I take that break. Maybe up and over the next ridge. I walk down the canyon, bears on my mind.

1984—Spanish Peaks, Montana

I lost the moose somewhere. No, there are the tracks. Once again I follow the winding trail of the cow and calf I've been watching the past hour. It's been a fun game for me. Watch from a distance, let them get ahead, then try to follow their trail to within sight again. We're going down the broad wooded canyon. I spend a lot of time up here but have never really explored the dense forest on this side of the creek. The going is getting tougher. Slower, too. Trees are growing closer together, and the downfall is thick in places. Where are those moose now?

The tracks are plain, but suddenly their trail has taken an abrupt turn. Instead of continuing down through the thick forest, they've turned back up the basin, climbing. I look at the tracks, then up the steep hill. Nope. Time to say good-bye to those guys. I'll just poke around in the trees for a time and then head home. I keep walking in the original direction.

Trees like matchsticks are all about me. The going is slow. Noisy, too. Limbs snapping. Legs crashing. Concentrating on getting over a log, I don't see the bear until he woofs. The direction I'm heading, I'd have bumped right into him in another thirty feet or so. He's standing. A jumble of fallen trees lie between us. My mouth open. Eyes wide. Grizz eyes staring me down.

He woofs again.

As I descend the canyon, the creek starts flowing off to my left. The sound is friendly, an endless babble. I'm just barely conscious of it. My thoughts are years old, focused on that standing bear. You're not supposed to run from bears. Like dogs, they chase things that move. So what did I do when that bear popped up in front of me? Why, I ran! In fact, I set new Montana speed records that day, bounding fifty yards farther away each time the bear woofed.

I'm smiling as I walk. Remembering. Kicking myself. Embarrassed at my sudden show of athletic ability that day. Wondering how I'd react today with some more years of experience and knowledge under my feet. Would I stand my ground? Or would I just run a bit faster?

Looking back, I know the bear was only trying to see me better, woofing to challenge my nearby presence and perhaps let me know I was too close. (I agreed.) A grizz can outrun a race horse. That one could have had me in seconds. Instead, he just observed my rather hasty retreat. My closest grizz encounter and I blew it.

Sometimes when I tell this story I leave off the running part. Wouldn't you? When folks ask what happened next, I tend to stretch the truth just a tiny bit.

"What happened then?" I repeat their question. Here I like to pause just a bit and look them seriously in the eye. "Why, that ol' bear . . . he ate me!"

I'm shaking my head as I hike out of Devil's Hole, letting the roar of Ledford Creek push me along. At a trail junction, I turn up the mountain. When I've gone a short way from the stream, I'm surprised by how quiet it gets.

The trail is a mess. By the tracks I can see that a herd of cattle has been driven through. The path is now twenty feet wide in places. All through the forest on the sides of it, the ground is churned up and trampled. Welcome to the wilderness?

I climb for a mile or so, take a short break, and climb again. The forest breaks open and suddenly I'm in a series of vast meadows surrounded by hundreds of cows. Cows in the streams. Cows in the forest. Cows in the clearings. Damn cows everywhere.

I have no great affection for cattle. For one thing, they're the stupidest creatures on the face of this Earth. Slugs are brighter than cows. Even politicians are smarter. (Well, on second thought, maybe cows aren't exactly the stupidest.) Maybe they're not to blame for this. Centuries of inbreeding surely have had some effect. Unfortunately, those centuries have affected us humans, too. It amazes me how much waste we allow in the name of the god-almighty cow.

Grazing in the West has had an overwhelmingly negative impact on hundreds of thousands of acres of public lands. Riparian areas are hit hardest. Too many unattended cattle devour streamside vegetation and trample the banks until entire watersheds are destroyed. Erosion is accelerated and water quality degenerates. The water warms up and fish die. Predators are poisoned and killed off for fear they might kill cows. Other wildlife is displaced from loss of habitat. Grazing has a domino effect, touching every other facet of life in the area. No wonder recent biological surveys have rated our public range as being in such poor condition.

Contributing to the problem, and creating another welfare state along the way, are extremely low grazing fees and many subsidies. When 98 percent of America's beef is raised on private lands, why should we allow degradation of our public lands by special interests? Things must change for the better if the West's wide open spaces are to be saved from desertification. We must learn to look at the bigger picture, respecting the other creatures that live on the land, protecting our riparian areas, and realizing that, yes, there are some areas that are just too fragile to handle the impact of cattle.

I like ranchers and respect their sense of heritage. I don't want to see their way of life totally disappear. Change is coming slowly. Some are becoming more responsible stewards of the public's land. They are learning new and better ways of treating the range. Fences are popping up along some of the stream banks to keep cows out. Non-lethal predator control methods are being introduced. Some ranchers are moving their cows more often so the herds will have less impact on the land. I just hope they can influence the rest of the industry to change the old ways before the land is irreparably damaged and before the backlash against irreverent grazing practices becomes a wave that puts them all out of business entirely.

I walk across the broad crest of the range, which is all open meadow. Cow shit everywhere. Cow tracks trampling everything. Cows everywhere. They stare at me. Empty blank faces. Four hundred pairs of eyes on me as I walk. Four hundred pairs of expressionless eyes, pondering.

In the middle of the mile-long clearing I stop, totally surrounded by the curious hoard. All is silent but for the gentle swish of four hundred tails. Why these mindless, locustlike bovines instead of sleek, wild creatures like elk, and grizz, and wolves? Something is swelling up within me. I can feel it coming. I can't help it.

"Yeeeehaaw!"

Arms flapping wildly, I dash forward into the mass of startled animals, screaming like a madman, loping like a gorilla. The air is suddenly a din of bawling cows and racing hooves. Dust is everywhere. The ground is shaking with the pounding of the fleeing herd. All around me cows are falling into each other, running in mass hysteria, insane fear and panic.

I love it.

I really do. I'm laughing and screaming, choking on dust and dung. The fleeing masses disappear over the hill. I slow to a walk, panting and satisfied. Kicks.

Friends Along the Way

It's the good hearts that spring from the salt of the Earth,
They inspire and brighten my days,
And I owe it all to the spirit of love,
And the friends along the way.
            —from the song "Friends Along the Way"

S ome mornings don't come soon enough. I've been anxious for this day to start. I was beat last night when I finally made camp. Eighteen miles yesterday. After a quick bath in the west fork of the Ruby River and a fast dinner, I'd gone right to sleep. The world could have ended. A bear could have hauled my tent away, with me in it. The river could have flooded, washing me to the Missouri. I know for a fact I would have slept right through it.

Yet I wake now with the first light, wide-eyed and fresh, ready to go. Today I'm meeting my Seattle friends, Tom Kwiatkowski and

Mary Hanneman, at a place called the Notch. They'll bring me a food drop and hike with me for a few days. It'll be good to see them. I wonder what the Notch will look like.

The morning is cool in the wooded canyon, but the uphill hike on a good trail warms me right up. I'm trucking like a semi, cruising up the grade, when a movement in the forest startles me out of my quick pace. A huge porcupine waddles purposefully up the mountain, her hind end nearly bare of quills. Her gait is slow but smooth, feet stepping with an almost dainty touch.

1975—Appalachian Trail, Vermont

The trail shelter is snug in the light rain. I'm dry and cozy in my sleeping bag on the big, wide sleeping platform. I have the whole lean-to to myself. The last light is nearly gone. I curl tighter and roll onto my side, dozing.

Something wakes me a short time later. What, I'm not sure. My eyes are open, straining to see in the half light. I don't want to move. Not yet. Better listen for a while.

There it is. Noise behind me. On the sleeping platform. Movement. Scraping. Humming? What the devil. Could another hiker have arrived in the dark? Why would he be mumbling and humming like that?

My stomach is starting to jump around a bit. Armpits are suddenly sweaty. I should roll over and look, but I don't want to. There, it's moving again. Oh, no! It's right next to me. Maybe if I lie still enough it won't see me. What is that humming? Gee, maybe it's some ax murderer humming with sick glee, getting ready to do his thing. I gotta look.

Quick as a rabbit, I roll over. The creature next to me freezes.

My eyes can make out its bulky outline halted in mid-stride. All is silent and still. Seconds tick by. A full minute. Then another. The humming starts. A nervous murmuring. I can't help it, I have to laugh. My burst of guffaws breaks the night. The porcupine retreats in a mad waddle into the darkness. I roll over and close my eyes.

A large doe is grazing on the trail ahead. Her ears are like wings. They flip this way and that, poised like radar as she studies me. She's a mule deer. It's no wonder where her species got that name. I take another step and she's off. As she runs, she spooks a red-tailed hawk. They cross paths, the silver morning light sparkling on each passing.

The Notch is a wide pass, open and marshy. The place is alive with elephant head and lush with grass, each blade glistening with pearly drops of dew. I follow the remnants of a jeep trail down the west side of the pass through the meadow. The Notch guard station stands empty and abandoned. No sign of Tom and Mary. Perhaps I'm too early, or maybe they've camped nearby. I tramp farther down the jeep trail. A tent comes into view. They're eating breakfast.

Up till now, I haven't spent much time with Tom, but I feel close to him. The first fan letter I ever received was from him. That was in '83. I still have the letter, and I wrote back. Over the years we've become good friends. We're a lot alike in the way we look at things, like wild country, the mountains, and grizz. Important things. Tom is a tall, lean man. With his short dark hair and trim beard, he looks like a scientist. He is in fact a physicist. He is also a man who loves the outdoors and spends much of his special time there, hiking and hunting.

Mary, his wife, is tall like Tom, light skinned while he is dark. She loves wild things, too. With a passion. They look good walking together with their packs bobbing.

We're walking back toward the Notch with full packs. I'm excited, and Tom and Mary are, too. We're heading up to walk the ridgeline of the Snowcrests. It's good to be with them. They have a fresh enthusiasm that is catchy. Each different flower is a new treasure for them. Each step brings a new adventure. Suddenly the mountains look different for me, too, this morning. I'm glad they've come to visit.

I've planned on an easy few days. It's tough to come from sea level, hoist a pack, and start walking up mountains. We pause a lot, but I don't mind. We pass through Honeymoon Park, and then hike higher. As I reach the upper ridge, breaking out of the trees, a coyote lopes nonchalantly over the crest. Excited, I yell to the others, then feel guilty that I'm so far ahead and have scared it off before they get there. Sure wanted them to see that coyote.

The flowers along the crest are a sea of color: lupine and phlox, prairie smoke, paintbrush, bistort, veronica, phacelia, and a host of others. Nearly all the ranges of southwest Montana are visible, as well as Red Rock Lakes, down in the Centennial Valley. The day is warm, but up here a nice breeze keeps it cool. We walk the open ridge, skirting the very summit of Stonehouse Mountain. With nonstop views we poke along.

The first night together we camp in a pretty basin. The trees are widely spaced with open meadows along a babbling creek. Lots of nearby springs, but the horse flies are numerous. They bite with a vengeance, and it hurts, too. It's worse when you're sitting still. They can find you easier, zero in on you like kamikazes. Usually they arrive in pairs, which makes me wonder, is it some kind of hunting tactic? While one is buzzing, distracting and drawing the swats, the other lights daintily upon the back of bare legs or goes for the choice spot of all, a shoulder blade. No notice of its presence until you feel the bite. Sneaky, but it works.

I smash them when I can catch them. But they have good timing, too—when one pair is gone, another arrives. To keep the flies at bay I go for a little exploratory trip of the upper basin, then take a bath before retiring to the tent to write in my journal.

Much later while we're cooking dinner, we notice a string of ravens flying over the ridge. They're heading west, one after another, soaring ever on and out of sight. A few minutes later the line is still coming. We're curious now and watch the procession go on and on, an endless stream. I've never seen so many of the birds. Where are they bound? What makes them want to move all together like that? Ravens are incredibly beautiful, intelligent birds, but because of their persistent scavenging ability, we often call them "dumpster chickens." I theorize that somewhere far to the west is the dumpster of all dump-sters. Come and get it!

An hour later the line of ravens begins to thin out. I'm sad to see the river of birds trickle to an end. I wonder if this was what it was like to see the last flock of passenger pigeons? Did they fly on and on, finally just fizzling to a line of lonely stragglers? A hollow, empty feel-ing sweeps through me. Oh, I know there are plenty of them. They're scavengers. They'll probably always do well. But the others of their kind, the creatures of the air, the songbirds and the waterbirds, con-tinue to lose ground, their nesting and feeding habitat lost to human crowding.

The last remnants of the flock have flown into the setting sun, when one lone straggler appears over the ridge on the trail of the oth-ers. How can he know where to go? Surely they must be out of sight by now. I watch the bird's solo flight across our little valley and into the vastness beyond, its wings flapping endlessly, a rhythm once traced, falling in timeless song, over and over. Black wings pumping away as the bird shrinks to a tiny speck. The last of the flock, a dark dot in the intensely clear Montana sky.

After dinner we hang our food. Tom and Mary have picked a good tree for theirs. I go over to watch. Directly under the hanging foodbag is a giant pile of bear scat. Must have been a huge bear. I point it out to them. They hoist the bag a little higher.

The horse flies disappear as the day cools to evening, but we're not left in peace. Mosquitoes take over. We call it a day and head for our tents. I'm snoozing before dark.

The dream's edges are dull and foggy. I'm not sure how I get there or where I am afterward. Somehow I am a bird. Not a large bird. Just an average one. It seems normal to be a bird. Everyone else is, too. I'm not even aware I am a bird until later, it feels so suited to me.

In the beginning I remember flying, but there were a few cages even then. They multiply fast. Soon I'm looking down on a world of cages. They cover the Earth. A solid mass of wire and metal, and not just one layer. The cages are hundreds of feet thick.

I don't know how it comes about, but suddenly I am in the cages, way down at the bottom, and the others are all here, too. I'm not sure how long we are there. It seems forever. Most of the birds become accustomed to their particular cage. I am always looking at the sky. You can just barely see it, way up there through all the wire mesh. For some reason I am always talking about, and looking for, the Great Firebird. I must really be babbling because after a time no one listens to me anymore.

Then one day I see movement in the skies. The heavens are suddenly filled with millions of birds swooping and soaring in wild flights of freedom. No one knows who they are. We are all the life on Earth, and we're still in our cages.

As we watch, a shadow falls over us. A sick dread flows down through every corner of my body. A giant eel-like creature flies amidst the hovering flock. First the one, then several more fill the sky. So awful, yet wonderful, too.

In a flash—I'm not sure if it's minutes or hours or days—I've ceased being afraid. I'm yelling, "The firebirds! The firebirds!"

Here the dream is misty and unclear. Somehow I begin to bore through the cages above me. One by one, I break through one wall of wire and then the next. It is hard, yet, I'm energized and strong.

Soon I'm breaking through the last barrier of wire. The air is a fresh blast that fills my heart, an elixir of ecstasy. I am flying! Laughing! Singing! The new birds smile at me. They nod like they know something I am just learning.

The firebirds are much higher than I can fly. I watch them wiggle and wave like flags in the heavens, scooting through the clouds. Each is a different color. The first one I'd seen had been blood red.

I look back down and see the Earth with its prison of cages coating every inch of its skin. With a shock I realize that no one else has followed me. I'm stabbed with fear. Much more than when I'd seen the first firebird.

Folding my wings, I dive faster than I've ever dived before, straight down through the holes I've bored, far down and back into the cage on the bottom I so recently left. I try to explain what is up there. My God, we can fly again!

No one wants to listen. My eyes fill with tears. My heart aches as if someone were tying a knot around it. I argue and plead. I beg. The cages are too comfortable. No one believes. No one wants to join me. No one wants to be free anymore.

At last, tears streaming, I fly back through the cages toward the sky. The firebirds are gone when I reach the open. I know they are gone for good. But the new birds still swoop and soar. I join them. The lightness I felt at first is gone, for each time I look down I cry. The Earth is still locked in its cages.

In the morning, the climb back up to the ridge is steep. We huff and puff our way out of Two Meadow Creek under cloudy skies. The breeze of yesterday is gone. All is still and quiet but for our passing steps. I get to the ridge ahead of the others. The wide, grassy crest rolls smoothly to the north and south. Inviting.

Waiting for Tom and Mary, thinking of how they walk together, I'm missing Leslie. She's on my mind a lot, but this morning thoughts of her fill my minutes alone on the open crest. Snug, cozy thoughts.

Funny, sexy thoughts. Anxious, missing-her kind of thoughts. I had no idea I would ever love her so much.

1986—BIG SKY, MONTANA

I come to the door. Shyly. Embarrassed even. The flower in my hand feels small and insignificant. I'm too conscious of it. I try to hide it at my side so know one can see. It's like a badge blaring "love." I wonder what she'll say, or even what she'll think. We were just friends. Nothing romantic between us. Nothing but hikes and talks and laughs. And now this. I'm bringing her a flower! I bet she'll laugh. God. What if she does?

This is crazy. I'm shaking, and my face is all red. At the door I knock. It'd be so easy to toss the flower now. She says to come in, and I open the door. Sweating. The stem of the flower crushed in my anxious hand. She's on the phone. She waves. I look around. I feel awkward, shifting my weight from one foot to the other, then finding a glass to put the flower in. She's smiling at me, talking on the phone.

Once we're all on the crest, we walk it for a few miles before dropping into Peterson Basin to camp. The place is beautiful. Grassy bowls, scattered stands of timber, and a few little streams. Unfortunately, there aren't many flat spots to pitch our tents. I walk around for over an hour before finally discovering an old camp with a fire ring and two flat spots. The bugs aren't as bad here. We don't miss them. It's a good spot, tucked among some Douglas fir and whitebark pine. A little stream flows down the hill. Elk are on the mountainside above. We like it.

After dinner we take a walk up through the trees to the upper meadow. We're quiet. The elk are up there somewhere. We get to the clearing, scanning uphill. A few bulls up there are looking down at us. The main herd can be seen behind them, just barely, like ghosts flitting over the forested crest.

Back at camp we get a fire going. I like a campfire. A lot of folks say they don't. They say it's not low-impact camping, you know, but I don't think they're being very honest. How could someone not like a campfire? It seems to me that fire touches something deep within us all. Something way back in there that recalls the essence of life. Something that knows just how sacred fire is.

I will admit that I have fires only when there's already a fire pit there. No sense in adding another black spot to the forest. Though I can and often do build a small fire to burn trash and toilet paper every few days, you'd never know the places I use for that. I'm good at reclamation.

Along those lines, I never bury my toilet paper. Nor do I burn it on site. I wrap it up and keep it in a plastic bag until I can burn it in one of my little fires. This way I can burn it thoroughly. None of this half-burned stuff lying around. None of this buried paper that the critters dig up and display at trailside.

A friend of ours is a guide. I won't mention her name because what I'm going to tell you is embarrassing for her. She leads folks through Yellowstone in the winter, bouncing along in snow coaches to get to some nice skiing. She points out the wildlife, explains some natural history, and generally awes the tourists with her vast knowledge.

One day she spotted a bird. "Bald eagle!" she pointed out. The coach came skidding to a halt as a dozen heads craned to see, binoculars poised, excited chatter upon every lip. The bald eagle turned out to be a raven. It had a wad of toilet paper in its beak. Disguised. You folks that leave your paper, beware!

But I'm talking about fire. We get ours going, and it lends a special feeling to our camp. It brings us closer together, a sharing and focus. We sit around as the daylight fades, talking. I pull out the guitar and sing a few songs. It's good singing by a fire. Some songs are made for that. Especially mine. Sometimes I can imagine the trees listening. Perhaps a coyote up the hill, ears perked and head tilted.

I'm just a half-blooded pup of a coyote,
Howlin' away my days.
Running to ground my star-studded dreams
And living my lone coyote ways.

The songs spill out with a new vibrancy. It feels right.

I went up on the mountainside to see what I could see
And the Vision that was given there, I carry on with me.
And I could see for miles and miles, and also unto Time.
And the Vision that was given there, was yours as well as mine.

We sing and talk. Talk and sing. The fire burns down, and we add some more wood. The evening is cool, but the fire warms us. The wilderness warms us, too. Being here together has linked us in ways that some people will never understand. Hearts are spilled, thoughts are shared. Wild country has a way of breaking down barriers between people. It strips us bare and reveals the inner core. When we finally head for the tents, it's with reluctance. This day could have been a bit longer.

~

This is my last day with Tom and Mary. We take our time with breakfast. In fact, we take our time with everything today. We're only planning on five miles.

The elk herd is across the canyon from the ridge we saw them on last night. After much climbing, we watch them from a high point of rock. They have no idea we're here. It looks like the perfect image of peace and quiet. Some lounge within the edge of the forest, others graze lazily in the clearing. A few calves leap and romp among the stillness.

We can also look out over the entire Peterson Basin. It looks like Ireland from here, green and lush. The Centennial Valley looks much more drab in comparison. The farther the view, the browner the vista. The crest of the Continental Divide, across the big valley to the south, seems very flat. I'll find out for sure in several days.

I've been watching Tom and Mary as they look out over the miles. They look content. They walk light and easy. I'm glad they're here with me. I didn't know what this stretch would be like, but I did know that I wanted it to be special. For them. These aren't spectacular mountains, but they are beautiful, and they are wild. Tom and Mary sense that. I see smiles on their faces sometimes when they're walking or looking out over the land. When you share a mile with a person, you share more than distance. I know why they smile. The time, the sights, the smells, the land itself all form a net of experience that binds you tighter to the mountain and to each other. These few days of wandering have cemented our friendship.

As we turn northward, we come upon ATV tracks. In this area, which is closed year-round to motorized vehicles, the ugly scars form a trampled line across the otherwise smooth, unbroken meadows. At the stream crossings and marshy areas, huge ruts have been dug with the fat tires.

The invasion of the destructive machines brings a dark cloud to the day. With all the miles of roads and land open to their use across this vast nation, they have come into one of our last trackless wild areas. These ATV folks are probably unaware of what damage they do, or of what destruction their big tires bring, but when it comes right down to it, they are true felons. The very character of the land is being stolen away. The stillness of the wild is shattered and broken with the noisy, exhaust-spewing machines. Glaring tracks (and trash) are left behind with no thought of the consequences. Precious fossil fuels are burned up in supporting this disrespectful intrusion of the wilderness. The land is wasted, and with it, the very peace that dwells only in these kinds of places. Why does everywhere have to be open to machines? Why can't we humans respect the last strongholds of wildness? Why can't we let them be?

One of my favorite bumper stickers: "American Wilderness: Love It, Or Leave It Alone."

Rain Walker

The clouds build up and the rain falls down,
Feeds the rivers, ocean bound,
Each wayward stream flows forth a dream,
An endless, dancing sound.

— from the song "Circle of Life"

Light rain last night. The patter on my tent is usually a welcome sound, but I'm planning a long day today. I'm not very happy with the misty morning. Leaving Tom and Mary is hard. We've had fun. Good talks and long laughs. We've gotten a lot closer. Hiking with someone does that. They've impressed me with their respect for the land. I've impressed them with my instant chocolate pudding.

A couple big hugs, and I'm off on my own again. They'll hike out to the Notch, completing a loop. I'll walk back up and over the crest we hiked two days ago, then head eastward. I have a rendezvous with Leslie at Red Rocks Pass in three days. It seems like a long ways from here. I'd better move.

Tom had wanted to see a moose. Several times he'd said, "I wonder if we'll see any moose today?" Or, "Wouldn't it be great if we saw a moose?" Fifteen minutes after I leave them, there she is. A big cow moose. It's funny how things work like that. Sure wish they could have seen that coyote back there, too.

The skies are gray. Totally overcast. Dripping mist. It feels good to be going uphill on a chilly day like this. Over to the west of me the clouds are hanging even lower, dragging bottom over the peaks and drooping into the valley. Each time I pause to look over that way, more of the mountains are gone.

From somewhere I hear a motor. My first thought is of the ATV tracks of yesterday. I'm pretty high up the ridge now, scanning the canyon below. Then I see it. And it is below me. A helicopter. The echo of the engine grows louder as it flies slowly back and forth in the canyon. Like I said before, this area is supposed to be closed to motorized vehicles. The helicopter sure sounds motorized to me. I watch from above as it slowly disappears up toward the Notch.

The ridge I'm walking is mostly meadow. There is no trail. It tilts upward at a gentle grade, leading me higher and higher. I don't know where it comes from, but suddenly the helicopter is flying down the ridge toward me. It passes once, within a hundred feet of me, then banks back and passes again. I keep walking, trying to ignore it. I'm steaming.

When the machine comes around again, I make a show of bending over to pick up a good throwing rock. I never look up at them. All I do is toss the rock up and down in my hand, looking at it. The chopper disappears over the next ridge.

The last of the trees are behind me now. The slope, grassy and studded with rocks, curves off into the mist. I could be in the moors of Scotland. Streaks of mist cloak the mountain. It feels like I'm starring in a spooky movie. A grouse takes flight at my feet. Scares the daylights out of me. Later, I see a few more. I'm watching for them now.

The peaks of the Snowcrest Range have been totally swallowed by the wave of clouds, but as I reach the narrow crest and the trail leading down the east side, the mountains begin to peek out of the mist. I take a short break. Just enough time to munch a candy bar and drink some water. It feels good to get the pack off for a minute. I've got a long day ahead of me. Have to, in order to get over to Red Rocks Pass in time to meet Leslie. Today is Friday. I'm meeting her on Sunday, and it's about fifty-six trail miles from here.

I'm heading down Divide Creek on a good trail now. Lots of big whitebark pine. Lots of deer, too. I'm a hiking fool. Steppin' out! My legs are feeling strong, and my boots are riding well. I feel like I can walk forever. Today I just might. The rain has held off, and the skies are hanging low and still. My steps sound extra loud today. Four miles, and the canyon spills me out into the open range. I can see for miles, rolling grassland and mountains with flattened tops of dense clouds.

I find Jones Creek and start following a jeep trail along its shallow course, farther away from the trees, farther from the mountains and into the vast open valley. I'm feeling very small, and though I'm walking at a steady clip, it doesn't feel like I'm making much headway. A beaver in the creek slaps its tail and dives. Sandhill cranes croak their distinctive call and take to the skies. I see many of these giant birds. They rise like pterodactyls and float slowly, effortlessly away. The call is one I hear over and over through these grassy miles. Each time I hear it, I pause in my stride and tilt my ears to listen. The cry fascinates me. It sounds old, old as the mountains, old as the rivers that have worn and shaped this valley. It touches me, striking something that makes me stop and nod as if I know some secret.

The jeep trail gets harder to see, fading into the grass and wildflowers. No worry, though. I can see where I want to go. Antelope race away. A golden eagle flies over the hills. My pace has a life of its own.

I cross the little dirt road running the length of the valley. Not a car in sight. Another jeep track goes east, up the other side. A light rain starts to fall. Out comes the blue pack cover and raincoat. Not a hard rain, at first, just a fine drizzle. Enough to soak everything. Enough to spark a wave of fresh smells, pleasant earthy aromas of wet flowers, sage, and grass.

The overgrown track leads me up into the foothills of the southern reaches of the Gravelly Range. Atop a nearby hill, two horsemen sit atop their mounts, still as statues, watching me. Perhaps they ponder on the blue thing walking toward them. My pack with the blue rain cover appears gigantic. I draw closer and wave. No response. Perhaps they'll ride down and talk. No. For ten minutes they watch and sit. Motionless. As I get within hailing distance, they turn and ride away down the other side of the hill. Friendly folks. It kind of bothers me.

A mile later I round the north side of a hill and find a few Doug fir. It's raining harder now, so I sit myself down in a dry spot under one of the big tilting trees. Time to put on the rain chaps. Munching some trail mix and looking at the map, I'm dry as can be in my little spot. A foot away the rain is soaking everything. It's really pounding now, and I'm so comfortable here. I'm not anxious to get wet, but after a time, I pull up my hood, hoist the pack, and set out. The rain does a tap dance on my rain gear. A little rivulet of water cascades down in front of my nose. The earth is dry. Even with as much rain that is falling, the ground just soaks it up. Thirsty.

I love it. I've come at least twelve miles and I am still feeling fresh. The scent of the wet, growing things fills me up. I can't get enough of these rainy day smells. I can almost hear the grass growing.

The jeep track leads me up and over a low divide, dropping to Fish Creek. The rain, already a downpour, turns up a notch and becomes a torrent. It's hard to see very far ahead. A shack appears out of the mist. It looks like it's about to fall over, but the roof is good. I step in. Marmot and mouse droppings cover the floor, the cupboard shelves, everything, but heck, it's dry. I clean off a chair, pull out a snack, and read a partially chewed *Life* magazine from 1970. Outside, it's not only cats and dogs, but badgers and bobcats, too. I mean, rain!

The rain slacks off after an hour to a mere downpour. Having finished with the *Life* and my lunch, I head out again, jumping across Fish Creek on a log. Soon, I come to Fish Creek Lake. It's a pretty good size for this part of the country, set in a bowl of barren hills. A jeep trail goes up the ridge above it. Now I hike into the clouds themselves. The misty grayness swirls about me, and I have no bearings at all. Can't tell if I'm going up or down. It's eerie. My world has shrunk to ten square feet. I'm walking slower, less confident about my direction. A deer bounds away in the fog. I'm not sure who is more startled, the doe or I.

JUNE 1976—LITTLE BELT MOUNTAINS, MONTANA

I'm walking carefully on this tiny track, hugging the side of the mountain as tightly as the fog draped over the forest. The clouds cloak the range this morning. I can see my feet clearly enough, but twenty feet ahead the world is murky grayness. All is still and quiet. I wonder what I'm missing. What exists thirty feet away from me? I could be passing right by the sight of a lifetime and not even know it. Mountain lions could be frolicking just down the hill. An elk could be calving just off the trail. I might be able to see for hundreds of miles from this grassy spot.

And then I see it. The bear's form looms out of the mist just ahead. A good-sized black bear, on all fours, looking at me. I've stopped, frozen to the trail, at first startled, but now curious. I guess he's a male. I don't see any cubs. Surely he will move on.

The bear is like a statue, as still as I am. Must be curious, too. He appears burly, but in the fog it is hard to say for sure. Dare I step closer? My feet inch up the trail another foot, eyes never leaving the hulking bear.

Hmmm. Still not moving, huh? I look into the dense mist on either side of the trail. As far as I can tell it looks steep both up or down. Might be tough to go around this fellow.

He still hasn't moved. Stubborn old bear. Weird that he isn't all that afraid of humans. Maybe he can't smell me. Surely he can't see me. I can barely make him out in all this fog. I know. I'll make some noise and scare him off.

I clap my hands. Loud.

I yell, "OK, Mister Bear, you can move on now!"

Nothing. No reaction at all. I edge a foot closer, then another. I clap again. Nothing. And then, suddenly, I can see him. Geez! I stomp boldly up, stand there next to him, then kick, boots thudding into a big stump.

A bear stump!

I'm walking faster, as if to hike away from the fool I've just made of myself. There are some great advantages to hiking alone, one of them being that no one can see all the goofy mistakes you make along the way.

One minute I'm hiking at full speed, the next I've come to a skidding halt. No, not another stump. Something is definitely moving on the slope above me. Something big. Something coming my way. For reasons that are evident, I'm sure it's a bear. My whole body is stretched taut, expecting. My legs are like tightly strung bows quivering in the chilly mist. It's coming closer.

I consider backing down the trail a bit. But I'm too curious (scared). Whatever it is doesn't know I'm here. The steps are not faltering one bit. And then, as if it were dropped out of the sky, a buck jumps onto the trail from the steep slope above. I almost laugh with relief.

The deer has paused, not fifteen feet in front of me, gazing down the trail, away from me. He tilts his head and sniffs but never turns around.

He cranes his long neck this way and that, looking for something he must sense. I feel like walking up and tapping his shoulder. "Excuse me, sir."

Finally, he lets out a sigh. His taut muscular body is suddenly relaxed. He bends down to nibble on some tasty treat. For several minutes he browses.

He's starting to walk up the trail and away when he finally throws a glance my way. Electricity! As if a charge has gone through him, he jumps—straight up!—then dances up the trail for a few yards before stopping to turn around. Now he studies me. Hard. I'm laughing out loud now. Who could help it?

My frightening appearance, so close in the mist, is tough on him, but I'm afraid the laughter is too much. He hangs his head and, with a little shake, starts to walk away. Three times I see him turn, looking at me, affirming that disbelief. My last glimpse is of him shaking his head in disgust, wandering into a fog so thick that it will hide even embarrassment.

I've come over a mile in the dense fog, now. Ahead the mist is thinning. A grove of aspen takes form. In a period of minutes it expands into an entire ridge, then a whole valley with Lower Red Rock Lake far to the south. The rain has stopped. Temporarily.

When I reach the west fork of the Madison River, I climb another ridge and drop into Tepee Creek, paralleling the river's route, but through a valley to the south. The base of the Centennial Mountains is visible now. Upper Red Rock Lake, too. All under a dense bank of clouds. I'm still feeling strong. The jeep trail I'm following makes the walking easy, and I'm making good time. Dozens of sandhill cranes take to the air as I make my way into the broad, grassy valley.

The place is peaceful. An old homestead, aged timbers a toasty brown, stands weathered and tilted. The years abandoned have been many, but at one time someone had put much work and care in here. I stop and gaze at the rough timbers, ax marks like fingerprints, visible and distinct. I feel a sadness here. Such a beautiful spot. So much work, so much care put into it. Gone. I wonder who they were. How long were they here? And where did they go? The years will bring it down, eventually. The wind and the deep Montana snows will help. Someday only the valley will remember the humans who came and tried to make a home.

Several miles later, I'm topping another ridge and beginning to drop to the river again. I've been seeing deer every mile. Now I spook a herd of seventy elk. At the river, a great blue heron poses like royalty. Just beyond is Landon Camp.

The old ranger station must have been a showplace in its day. The one-room white clapboard cabin was at one time surrounded by a picket fence. Now everything is falling down. The place is in disrepair, and trash abounds in the yard. Swallows, hundreds of them, swoop and chirp as I get closer. They've nested in the eaves and under the porch roof. I walk through the cloud of birds and into the cabin. Marmot scat is everywhere. Trash is here, too, but the roof is good and the windows are intact. There's a wood stove. Outside the rain has just stopped again. I contemplate going on. It would be easy just to continue, find a place to camp, use the tent tonight. But now that I'm stopped, the miles of the day come rushing upon me. Twenty-eight miles. More than half of it in the rain. The temperature is dropping. The wood stove appeals to me.

I put the broom to good use, giving the cabin a clean sweep. It takes a while. The mattress on the bunk, I sweep and turn over. It looks good on this side. Each time I go outside, the swallows get excited. At first, I walked with ducked head. Now I'm getting used to it.

The wood stove is going. A bat flew out of the chimney when first I lit it, then disappeared in the tiniest crack between the wood and the brick mortar. I've got my clothes rinsed and drying. Water's on for tea. I'm curious about the cupboards. Opening one, I see it's full of empty bottles and nails. Another has a petrified box of brown sugar. I bend over to open the big lower one. The door swings open and looking up at me is one of the fattest marmots I've ever seen. It startles me, and I slam the door shut before I realize what it is. Then, more slowly this time, I open it again. She's still there, curious and a bit peeved, too, at the disturbance.

All evening I occasionally step over to the "marmot cupboard" and open it. If I'm noisy, she escapes down a hole chewed in the floor, but mostly, she just stares at me until I close the door. I'm thinking of all the wildlife I saw today. It doesn't stop.

In the morning a loud crash on the porch awakens me. I sit up with a start and listen. Nothing. The cabin is as still as ice, frozen silence, but for the distant murmur of the west fork. Later, I arise and open the door to find one of the swallow's nests has fallen directly on the doorstep. Several dead baby birds lie there at my feet, tiny pink bodies twisted in a pile.

I think of those little snuffed-out lives a lot as I walk today. I witness death fairly often in the wilderness. It is not a foreign thing here. It's not unusual to find the carcass of a deer, or to witness a hawk swooping to take a mouse, a coyote pouncing on a ground squirrel. The fuel that keeps the whole thing going is based on death. One creature's passing is another's birth. Nothing goes to waste.

We Americans are used to waste, swamped in violence, immersed in graphic portrayals of pain and misery. Television and cinema define our culture. We soak up more death and dying in one evening of entertainment than most veterans see in an entire military career. But that's all in "fun." When it comes down to the real thing, we as a whole tend to be strangers to anything having to do with death. Oh yes, we see it in sterile hospitals and in "life" on the big screen, but what of the natural evolution of our own bodies back to the earth from which they come?

I wonder what's on Mom's mind these days. What thoughts come to her as she fights her biggest battle? I wish I'd had the courage to ask her when I was there. Does she ever wonder just where her disease comes from? Does she contemplate where it might lead her? I watch a snake eating a gopher with interest, yet I couldn't ask my own mother about her thoughts on dying.

We humans are a funny species. We can't look death in the eye, yet we accept the environmental degradation and poisoning that breeds cancer. I don't get it. We depend on technology to fix everything (including us), yet that very technology continues to poison our health and our home. Something isn't working.

~

The clouds are hanging in the canyon. It's icy cold. I set off wearing my wool sweater, and it takes two miles to warm up enough to take it off. Nippy! The trail I'm on follows the slow-moving river. Actually, right here it's more of a creek than a river. In this country, though, water is a big thing. Hence, bodies of water get tagged with big words. Calling it a river is like a promise; a hopeful promise that lies between the sage-covered hills and the lush creek bottoms. A promise of things to come. A promise of the life to be. A river is a precious thing, even if it is a creek-sized one.

A great blue heron rises from the mist-covered willows. Its wings, like giant sails, flap a slow, steady wave. Legs dangle, forgotten. The sharp beak, a rising arrow, pierces the morning chill. Silently the huge bird gains the skies, a god blessing the morning.

Coyotes are yipping. Cranes croaking. Moose graze in the willows. Warblers sing here, too, and deer stroll up in the pines. Hawks scream overhead. The place is alive. The sun has burned away the fog, and dew drops glisten like prisms at the end of each blade of grass. The sun feels good on my bare arms. The place feels good in my heart. I don't feel the least bit hurried. In fact, I'd rather just sit and soak things in. Yesterday's miles are catching up with me.

Eventually I turn toward Hoodoo Pass on a pleasant trail leading me through scattered meadows and a healthy forest. How special this little canyon is. How lucky I am to take this route. It's a perfect day. A golden eagle screams overhead. I look up, straining to catch a glimpse of the circling raptor. It screams again, the cry echoing a warning off the surrounding hills. My trail suddenly merges onto a logging road. Up the slopes lies the barren ground of clear-cuts. An eerie silence hangs over the canyon here, perhaps a sense of waiting to see what comes next?

I stop, but then hesitantly come wholly into the cut. I'm not aware of having taken the pack off but find myself sitting on a new stump, my head in my hands. The trees still standing at the edge of the cut look so green, so vibrant, and so full of life. I study the healthy trunks, the smooth bark, the needles soft and leathery. The life there is rich, reaching out to something within me, to something all around me. But as I shift my gaze, that part of me begins to shrivel and dissolve.

Here the ground is laid bare, tossed and trampled, cut and gouged. Stumps and trees are laid to waste, lying tossed haphazardly without care. Many of the trees have not been taken. They're bulldozed or cut down and left to rot, sometimes to be burned in a slash pile later. The place reeks of violence. The amount of waste and blatant disrespect for the land is written boldly in such a picture. Nowhere is humankind's fear of nature displayed more openly. Nowhere, is the destiny of the planet's wildlands so chillingly projected. The clear-cut. I choke on the word.

I'm thinking of the growing number of clear-cuts I've witnessed in the Northern Rockies over the past decade. It has become an epidemic of astounding proportion. I shift my perch atop the stump. The trees lie scattered and crushed about me. Why can't logging be done with more wisdom and respect? We have laws in this land dealing with abuse. If folks abuse their children, the kids are taken away and given a better home. If folks abuse their dog, the creature is taken away. Why do we allow people to abuse the very Earth we live on? If private lands are abused, why not remove ownership when the land is being degraded? When public lands are in such a situation, isn't it time we cleaned house and really looked at the way our federal lands are being mismanaged? Why do we humans destroy the most beautiful, the most fragile, the most wild? What is it that makes us ignore and downplay the existence of other creatures' needs? Why can't we keep our hands off these last bits of wild country? The answers lie somewhere within all of us. I shoulder the pack and move on, my steps slow and heavy.

Hidden Lake lies tucked in a glacier-carved valley, a picture-perfect kind of place. The kind of place you dream of going to when you think of a Montana mountain lake. Leslie and I hiked over from Cliff Lake earlier in the summer. We had a picnic, went for a quick dip, and watched the abundant birdlife that abounds along the lake's shores.

After walking a few miles of clear-cuts, I'm looking forward to a peaceful camp in the hills near the lake's shore. I can picture myself lounging naked in the grass after an icy dive into those clean waters. I could use a bath. The sun is shining. The gloomy mood of the wasted forest is slowly starting to lift. I'm pounding down the trail to the perfect camp spot I know is there.

There are few disappointments in life as great as having a special campsite, knowing it is there, longing for it, picturing it, walking fifteen miles to get to it, and then having someone else camped there when you get to it. My spot is taken. Today is a Saturday. I'd overlooked that fact. I'd forgotten the dreaded invasion that often comes to the mountains on that day in the summertime. The quiet, deserted lake I've been walking toward is nowhere to be found. In its place is a hopping hodgepodge of hikers and fishermen. Fishing poles bristle like porcupine quills. Float tubes and rowboats dot the lake. Everyone is obviously here to "get away from it all."

I should hike on over the ridge. I admit I'm disappointed by all this zoolike behavior, but I also admit that at the same time, all this activity has me intrigued. I feel drawn to this place like all the others, all the "someone else"s. Let's face it. We're social critters. I'll hang around and watch.

I end up camping on the south end of the lake. The campsite is littered with the debris of countless weekend warriors. Toilet paper, broken bottles, empty cans, cigarette butts, and bits of tinfoil cover the site. A number of fire rings, some within a few feet of the next one, dot the area. It's a sad place, but I'm determined to see this through. It takes me two hours to clean the place up.

Even with all the folks around, I know I'll be able to enjoy the lake. I prop my ensolite pad and sleeping bag against a tree and settle into the cozy nook. I'm just getting comfortable, just relaxing into my favorite power-lounging position, when a stream of curses and splashes crashes through the peace of the summer day. A group of fishermen paddle their float tubes nearby. A steady barrage of insults and swearing bounces across the calm waters of the lake.

1974—Appalachian Trail, Maine

Echoes are amazing things. They can inspire. They can awe. They are the trick up the sleeve, the coups de grace, the icing on the cake, the most dramatic of Ma Nature's sound effects. I'm camped at Daisey Pond, in one of the little trail shelters. A young couple with a few kids are camped nearby. It's after dinner, and we're all down by the pond. The air is still, the forest mirrored perfectly in the glassy surface of the pond. We skip rocks. The kids are getting the hang of it. The ripples go on and on.

Another 2,000-miler walks up the trail. I know he's a long-distance hiker before he says a thing. After months on the trail myself, I recognize the look. He's lean and tan, shaggy hair and scraggly beard. He hikes in shorts (shorts that are wearing thin) and a dirty, sweat-stained T-shirt. It's the typical uniform of the end-to-ender. His name is Joe. He doesn't talk much. I think he's in a hurry to get to Katahdin. We visit briefly and he hikes on. I go back to skipping rocks with the nice family.

Fifteen minutes later, Joe's hiking partner arrives. Have we seen Joe? Yes, he just passed by. One of the kids spots Joe on the other side of the lake. On the wrong trail.

"There he is."

Joe's partner cups his hands to his mouth. "Hey, Joe!"

It echoes endlessly across the lake. "Joe, Joe, Joe, Joe, Joe . . . ."

We all marvel at the sound. The kids have looks of awe written on their little faces. Dad says, "Listen, Johnny! It's an echo!"

We see the tiny figure across the lake come to a stop. Joe's partner hollers again.

"Hey, Joe! Joe! Joe! Joe! Joe! . . ." It bounces across the lake and keeps going. We all look at each other. Wow, what an echo!

"What? What? What? Wha? Wha? Wha? . . ." Joe yells back.

And this is even better. The words are clearer. They boom stronger and echo longer, on and on. We're all grins. Mom is saying, "Isn't that wonderful?" The kids are eating it up.

"Where you going? goin? goin? goin? . . ." Joe's partner yelling again.

Dad says he wishes he had a tape recorder. The kids are spellbound.

"To Katahdin Stream! Stream! Stream! eam! eam! . . ."

I've never heard such a perfect echo. We're all oohing and aahing with each word bounced off the pond. Mom, Dad, and the kids are applauding.

"You're on the wrong trail! trail! trail! ail! ail! . . ."

This is really something. Amazement is written on the kid's faces. Mom says, "Oh, isn't this nice?"

There is a pause. A dead, silent stillness slips back over the lake. We're standing, leaning toward the pond's edge, expecting.

Waiting, all ears. Intrigued adult ears, and tiny, questing child ears. And then it comes. Joe's final answer.

"F#&*k! F#&*k! F#&*k! F#&*k! F#&*k! uk! uk! uk! . . ."

The loud fishermen dominate the lake for a few hours. I don't understand such folks. Why bother coming to such a peaceful, quiet place if not to savor that which the lake offers? Should the visitor not respect his host's home? Leave your baggage at home! I feel like yelling, You've already left your brains!

I read and nap away the afternoon. I never see the loud ones leave; I'm just conscious of it. A great peace suddenly cloaks the lake. It sweeps swiftly through the water, the forest, and the soft lighting of the parting day. And through me.

I hesitate to breathe. Such quiet. Thoughts, deep in my brain, seem loud. I try not to move, as if one false step could shatter the precious glass, the frozen silence that is the lake. The absence of sound is not a void, for this silence is full and overflowing, and deep as the mountain. My ears strain for sound above and through the northern skyline of forest. Far below the ice-smooth surface of the lake, down to the silty bottom of its darkest depths, nothing moves. The lake owns itself. Again.

~

I want you to understand something about walking, something about long-distance walking. It's not a physical kind of thing. Oh, there's the rhythm, the sweat, the power of your legs chugging away. That's a thing most of us can comprehend, and that is indeed very physical, but most folks think of these long hikes as a feat of some super being. If you could see me, you'd know the truth. I'm tall and skinny. I'm not an athlete. I'm not in any way, shape, or form a super hiker. The physical part of the trek is real and demanding, but more important, I think, is the will. When it comes right down to it, walking is often a state of mind. Many days are a trial for me physically, yet because of my intense desire to be there, the miles drift by undetected. Often, it seems, sheer willpower pulls me over a mountain.

As in anything, one must be intent upon the path. When you're unhappy about The Way, that's when The Way becomes difficult. A long trek is a journey through the land, but it is also a searching odyssey into your self. It is not for everyone. To be alone and facing the wild places on their own terms is often easy compared to looking into our true selves for weeks and months at a time, which being alone on the trail forces us to do. But it's often the connection with the wilderness that pulls us through the confrontations within ourselves. I wouldn't want to be alone for so long in any other kind of environment.

But these are just outlines. What of the actual steps? When does walking, the motion, become thought? This is what I want you to understand. There is a point where the action goes unrecognized and is replaced by an emptiness that is based totally in the present. It is a knowledge, gained in each step, flooded with each turn, and brought into being for each second of the day. It is a holy state. This is when I wish I could tap myself, pouring my essence into a bottle. When

99

someone asks me, "Why do you walk?" I'd just pull out the brew and say, "Drink this." Some days I can feel the miles building up under me, piling up and spilling over. But then there are days, like this one, when I float in a blessed euphoria. Steps cease to be merely feet gained. Rather, each action is a journey of its own. Each step holds its own wonders. And joy floods me at every turn.

I'm walking at first light and already there are two fishermen on the lake. These guys are the real thing. They stand frozen in the rising mist, poised like egrets, studying every inch of water before them, statues waiting patiently for life.

After climbing a steep escarpment above the lake, I walk a rolling plateau with mixed stands of aspen and fir, and broad, sweeping grasslands. The sky is clear and the day is cool. If I stop to watch the deer, or the far peaks, goosebumps will appear on my bare legs. I keep moving. It's a joyous time to walk, to be here and part of the morning.

Gradually the clear sky gives way to full floating, shiplike clouds. A cool breeze keeps the hiking pleasant. Near Saddle Mountain a group of five bull elk break from the shelter of the aspens, massive racks tilted back over rippling muscle. Their movement is smooth and graceful. Huge antlers, waving and rocking, disappear over the hill.

By midday I find myself on the Continental Divide. It's low, with a gentle, rounded contour at this point. Starting down a jeep road, I notice a Continental Divide trail marker. And then another. It excites me. In fact, just being on the Great Divide excites me. This ridge runs for thousands of miles north and south, through the continents of North and South America. Upon its crest, the rainfall is funneled into streams tumbling down the east side toward the Atlantic Ocean, or on the west side bound for the Pacific. It is the divide of these two immense watersheds. The spine of a continent.

I know these miles, or at least some of them. In 1979 I walked from Mexico to Canada following the divide. Five additional long walks have led me along various sections of its rugged mountains over the years. Now it feels like an old friend, a friend I feel comfortable with. I'll be walking with this friend for the next few weeks.

Antelope play and run among the grassy slopes. The Centennial Range is getting closer—magnificent, green and rugged. The little track I walk is dropping me lower with each mile. I'm starting to get dry. Hungry, too. It's time to take a break. but I'm too close to Red Rock Pass now. I'll be seeing Leslie any minute. She'll come driving up this dusty trail in her pickup. Or maybe she'll be parked and waiting at the pass. I'd best push on.

But the day remains quiet. No sign of her. No sign of anyone. The county road is a strip of silent gravel when I reach it. The pass is empty. Stepping onto the packed dirt road, I look long in both directions. Nothing—except the dog.

East of me, in the middle of the dusty lane, a lone black mongrel sits regally, gazing toward the mountain to the south. The dog is as dusty as the road. His thick, shaggy coat is tangled and matted. There's no doubt he has traveled far. He spots me and immediately retreats farther down the road. I call out, coaxing. He walks slowly toward me, curious. Ten feet away he sits down. If I approach he moves away. As long as I'm in one spot standing still he'll come back, but not closer than ten feet. I give up and cross the road.

Propping my pack in the shade of a tree, I gobble my trail mix and gulp some much-needed water. The few peanuts I toss to the dog disappear in little snaps of his jaws. Like a coyote chomping grasshoppers, the dog clacks his teeth at the tiny bits. When I'm done eating he gradually moves off.

I read and doze. A car drives by. Twenty minutes later, another. A battered pickup truck stops near the sign proclaiming the Continental Divide. I'm sitting in the meadow nearby but feel invisible. I know they don't see me. The time in the backcountry has given me a closeness to the land that helps me blend in.

Dad gets out to pee on one side, Mom on the other. The four or five kids spill over the sides of the truck's bed, squatting here, squirting there. The dog wanders over, slowly drawn to laughing kids' voices.

"Looks like you've had a hard day," says Dad to the dog.

"Can we keep him?" A little boy's first thought.

Dad ignores the question. "Give 'em a chip, Ru."

"Nice doggie! Can we take him home, Dad?" Ru is committed to this idea.

"Give 'em a chip, Ru." Dad likes the idea of feeding the stray rather than taking it home.

"He likes it! Can we take him home, Dad?"

I give it to the kid, he is persistent.

"Give 'em a chip, Ru." So is Dad.

They drive off without ever answering Ru's question. The black dog stands in the empty road all alone, licking the chips from his teeth.

Later, I walk into the forest, looking for a campsite. When I come back to wait for Leslie, the black dog is gone.

Thirsty Miles

Once in a while you'll find a friend
Where the memories meet at the rainbow's end.
Though life goes on, I'm glad for the thought
Of the gift you gave, and the peace you brought.
                    —from the song "Once in a While
                              You'll Find a Friend"

I'm walking the county road through Alaska Basin. The sun is rising behind me, its rays warm and pleasant on my back. I'm not carrying the pack. My legs step out long and lightly without it. The valley is still and silent but for steps crunching loudly on the gravel road.

Last night was another rendezvous. First came Leslie with Biff Schlossman, prepared to hike through the Centennials for a few days. They came bouncing up in the truck, all grins, leading another car with Brick and Margi Root and their one-year-old son, Bridger. Biff and the Roots are all dear friends. These visits from so many friends along my trail is a nice change of pace. We ate giant burritos around a tiny campfire, caught up on each other's stories, and laughed and sang into the night. Their presence is a big hug of assurance.

Now I'm walking the road. A fox runs across ahead of me, low to the ground, bounds into the field, and is gone. Leslie and Biff drive past in the truck, my pack in the back with theirs. Brick and Margi zoom by behind them. They'll set up a shuttle, park the truck at Odell Creek, where Leslie and Biff will end up in a few days, and meet me a couple miles down the road with the loaded packs. I didn't want to make them walk the road, yet wanted to keep the continuity of the trek. I wave and keep on walking.

I'm walking fast. Don't want the others to have to wait. The faster the legs go, the further my thoughts ramble. Images skip through my brain, crowded and changing like the flowers dotting the roadside: sandhill cranes croaking in the distance; Biff singing "Nightrider's Lament" last night; a dead snake squashed flat. I wonder if we'll get rain today. My legs feel strong. More images: watching little Bridger teeter along holding Leslie's hands; Mom holding me on a bicycle, pushing from behind (How far back was that?); clouds hanging on the west end of the valley poised like vultures; (I wonder about Mom); a red-tailed hawk screaming; Leslie mad at me for being gone; the weasel up ahead running furtively across the road; Brick and Margi off for some sea-kayaking. Those clouds look mean. I think those far hills are where I walked yesterday morning. Damn cows where antelope should be. Biff sounds better each time I hear him sing. Leslie was so mad. I was mad because she was mad. It was so silly. It's a good day for walkin'. But those clouds . . . .

Leslie and Biff are all smiles, sitting on the roadside atop a pile of packs. I could make out Biff's grin a long ways down the road. It's kind of a beacon. He's dark, anyway, and tan from being outside. His smile radiates like neon. He wears it well, and often.

Biff's a musician, too. Knows more songs than anyone I know, a walking library of tunes. We share good finds, new songs we really like. Books, too. He comes knocking on the door, always kind of shy but blurting out what new song he's just learned. I pass him the guitar and off we go.

He's a man of wild inconsistencies: a quiet bookworm, sensitive, a man who loves to be in the wild places by himself; yet, he's also a party animal. There isn't a bar in this corner of Montana that doesn't know him. In a lot of ways he and his battered guitar, his car held together with duct tape and bumper stickers, and his raging thirst for fun have become legendary. Of all the things we've shared over the years—songs, laughter, thoughts, books, drinks, and dreams—the thing I've always wanted to share with him most is what we are about to share now: a few days on the trail.

We hoist the packs, climb a fence, and walk slowly up a narrow two-track. It feels good to get under way. With so many folks, doing so much this morning, we get a much later start than usual. We joke and chat an endless stream. The threatening clouds to the west of us are building, but we'll take it as it comes.

We leave the track after a mile and a half, climbing through a clear-cut and then making our way up a steep yet magnificent ridge. Higher and higher we climb, puffing and sweating, calling out to each other at every new flower, every new sighting of some wild treasure.

The moment of breaking from the trees, of grasping the view below us, is a moment of pure joy. Oh, we knew it was coming, eventually, but when we are hit by the spaciousness and the sudden range of sight, the wide vista becomes a fuel. The fatigue that we all felt after the steep climb is gone. In its place is a rush of awe and excitement, a zest to keep on to see what's next. I've felt this inexplicable burst of energy before, usually in the mountains. The views keep you going.

The storm misses us. We can see it storming a couple miles away, hitting the Snowcrests. A cheer from us, and we walk on, following the open ridge higher. In no time we're cresting the Continental Divide again. This is always a special moment for me. I look left and right, expecting to see a lone hiker, an end-to-ender, a Mexico-to-Canada hiker. Maybe some other day. Today we have this part of the divide all to ourselves.

We're standing in Idaho now, looking south. Island Park Reservoir is down there, and the endless lava flows of the Snake River Plain to the southwest. I study the empty plain stretching into a hazy distance. I've walked that desert. I won't walk there again. That's one place I've trekked where I can say that for sure.

"Look, the Tetons!" Biff is saying. Sure enough, to the east, and south a bit, the Grand Teton seems closer than ever. What a range. The sight is riveting. Named by some horny Frenchman over a hundred and fifty years ago, a man I assume enjoyed big-breasted women;

they exude a charm all their own. The mountains, that is. We stand there a long time, silent, just looking, but the barren plain keeps drawing my gaze.

The crest of the divide has no path here, but we can easily follow the ridge. I'm surprised to find CDT (Continental Divide Trail) markers. The little blue and white markers appear atop posts. We see a few of them, spaced every quarter mile or so, before they disappear. Back in 1979, when I walked the Continental Divide, there wasn't any real trail. Each person who hiked it, and there weren't very many, determined his or her own route, linking up various trails with lots of compass work. I liked it that way. Who needs a trail when you have a ridge like this to follow?

Nowadays, things are changing. There are guidebooks out, each with different routes, and the Forest Service has gotten into the picture, trying to define where the official trail should go, constructing new trails into heretofore unvisited, one-of-a-kind country. New trails in some places bother me. Oh, don't get me wrong. Trails are nice to hike on. I love trail walking. And I think America should have an extensive trail system. At one time the trails in our national forests extended over five times the miles they do today, and I think many of those trails should be revived.

The thing that worries me is this mad obsession to put the human hand into every nook of every corner of every last vestige of wild country. We must leave some areas untracked. We must leave some far corners where the land is king; places where wilderness travelers may go, but where they must go on the land's terms, not on some fancy, graded trail. We must leave long ridgelines, and hopefully long stretches of the Continental Divide, where a hiker can taste the freedom of finding the way without the aid of this tiny strip of civilization we call a trail.

The markers disappear, but we keep to the crest of the divide, making our way up and over a series of wooded knobs. The saddle where I had thought to make our first night's camp is a jumble of dense trees and rocks. We turn down Schneider Creek, on the Idaho side, and find a well-protected flat spot in a forest of lodgepole pine.

Our campsite is perfect but for one minor detail. No water. We grab the waterbag (it holds nearly three gallons) and our water bottles, all empty, and start down the canyon. In these mountains we won't have to go far to find water. At least that's what I tell Les and Biff.

A mile later, we're still descending a dry canyon.

The canyon is pretty, lots of big trees and wildflowers everywhere, but it's hot, too. And we're dry, and getting drier. Just the idea of not having water makes our mouths parched. This is strange. Surely, we'll find some soon. Let's go around this next bend. If we don't find any then, we'll go back. Try somewhere else.

Around the corner is just as dry, but the next bend looks more promising. Well, OK. We'll push on around that next one, but if there's no water, we'll really turn back.

This canyon baits us again and again, around the next bend and the next, luring us lower and lower down the mountain. Finally, we sit down. It was a grunt getting up to the divide this morning. We're tired and thirsty. And now we have a long hike back up to our camp. I don't have the map, but I remember a spring shown on it to the east of us, up the trail we passed a ways back. I think. The others are skeptical, as well they should be, but I remember it. It's a sure thing. No telling how much farther we'd have to go down this canyon to find water. We turn and head back.

1983—Snake River Plain, Idaho

Should I turn back? It's only eleven miles back to the cave. There's water there for sure. But eleven miles? That will kill this day, and part of tomorrow. Of course, it might kill me if I don't go back. I'm nearly out of water.

This is a fierce desert. No shade. Even the sagebrush is stunted. Hundreds of square miles of barren, open plain, lava flows and sage. I passed the last scruffy juniper a few miles back. And it's hot. July is not the greatest time to be wandering around out here. This is crazy. But I'm walking the length of Idaho this summer. Yesterday I did a twenty-eight-mile day to get to this wild stuff. I got what I asked for. Here it is.

The Great Rift runs through this plain, an old volcanic vent, a crack in the Earth's crust forty miles deep. Millions of years ago this plain was a sea of molten lava. Today the lava is still here, frozen in waves, solidified in pools, twisted into sharp, bizarre shapes.

The plain is beautiful in its way. The sweep of miles, spaciousness smooth and unbroken, stretches as far as the eye can see. The pale greenish gray of rabbit brush and sage is dotted with the black of the lava outcroppings. Humankind is but a visitor here. No one lives in this place. Even the Native Americans and mountain men, those who never thought twice about venturing into every nook and cranny of the West, made it a point to steer clear of this plain. They'd go a hundred miles out of their way to avoid crossing it.

But here I am. And here, too, on the southern edge of this unusual land is a water tank. This is shown on my topo map. This is where I was planning on my last water stop. This is why I didn't fill up my water bag eleven miles back.

I'm sitting in the narrow band of shade provided by the big green tank. I've been here a couple hours. Bummed. I can't get any water to come out of the big hose. I turn the dials, the various spigots, but nothing happens. It must be empty. And it's so hot, I'm drinking more water than I'd planned.

I've been sitting out the hottest part of the day. It's late afternoon, and I've got to make my move. No point in going farther north. My water bottles are nearly empty. I'd best walk back to the cave. I can be there before dark, easy. The clouds are building in the west. It'll be cooler walking now. I stand and stretch. Maybe I should try these knobs again. I bend down and give them another crank. And another. There is a distant sound, deep within the tank. What have I done differently? A stream of water, four inches wide, is suddenly gushing from the hose. Without hesitation, I step under the cool, clear water, clothes and all. Afterwards, I fill my bag and water jugs. When I leave the water tank, I'm walking north into fifty miles of dry country. My pack is heavy, loaded with the water I hope will see me through.

The walk over the ridge to the spring seems longer than it is. We're tired and want to be in camp, but at least my memory of the map is correct. We find the spring. Its flow is strong, the water so cold it hurts your teeth. We drink and fill the water bag and various bottles. After a short rest we head back to camp, trading off on the job of carrying the now-heavy water sack.

My pack feels like I'm carrying half an ocean. But now that I've got as much water as I can carry, I feel confident about making it across the *plain in good order. I'm walking at a good clip. The clouds to the west of me look like trouble. I wanted to walk until dark, since it's so much cooler, but this brewing storm could throw a wrench in that plan.*

A while later I'm marveling at the immense black cloud growing on the western horizon. It's a living thing, growing higher every ten minutes. Already twenty miles long, it now stretches thousands of feet up into the sky. It's a frightening sight. The eastern edge of the cloud is sheer, like a cliff. I've never seen anything like it, a dark wall, advancing faster and faster over the plain. Toward me.

Lightning is flashing now. Still miles away, the tongues of light dart across the distant darkness, silhouetted against that ominous cloud. The wind picks up. I'm walking as fast as I can under the heavy pack. I don't know where I'm going, but I want to get there before the storm hits.

A mile later and the wind is howling. The thunderclaps are closer. Louder, too. The cloud is bigger, and darker, than ever. I can't get over how straight and sharp the eastern edge is. It's a wave, without a curl. It's a knife, the lightning, its teeth. It's a living thing that moves like a predator, stalking the plain.

A mile later, I can barely stand in the wind. The cloud is nearly upon me. I feel like a little rowboat on a vast ocean about to be rammed by a huge ocean liner bearing steadily down upon me. One lightning bolt follows another. The thunder cracks and roars. I'm a little nervous, a mite uneasy. Hell, I'm scared shitless.

I'm frantically trying to put my little tent up. It's a tiny one-man thing, a tube of Gore-Tex–coated fabric with a couple low hoops. The wind makes putting it up difficult, but I'm moving fast. The mass of the storm breathes down my neck like a charging grizz.

The tent is up. I toss in the pad and sleeping bag, grab my pack, move it nearly thirty yards away, and put the raincover over it. Don't want that metal pack frame too close to me right now. I feel the first drop of rain and slide myself feet first into the tent. Not much room, like an arm going into a sleeve, but it's cozy. And at least I'm low to the ground now. I'm willing myself smaller and smaller as the cloud passes over me.

Each bolt of lightning feels like it's right next to me. The thunder is shaking the Earth. My eyes are closed tight. I can't shrink myself small enough. I always used to dream of being a mountain goat, but right now, life as a mole wouldn't be too bad.

The rain, the intense downpour I know is coming, never does. Instead, the lightning and thunder continue a constant crack and rumble. Gradually I relax, falling asleep to the roar of the storm.

The silence awakens me.

I crawl out of the tent into the stillness. It's nearly dark. The lightning flashes are miles away. The storm has passed, but something is wrong. There is a smell. Smoke. The night air is heavy with it. And then I see it, far to the west. Flames on the horizon. A grass fire. I remember talking to a BLM employee from these parts last winter. He had warned me about the fierce heat of this place in July. He had also told of the severe lightning storms and the resulting grass fires, which can sweep for miles across the plain. Until now, I had forgotten the conversation.

Back in the tent, I try to go back to sleep. I can't tell how far away the actual fire is, nor can I tell which way it's burning. Chances are it's coming my way because of the earlier wind, but I do need some sleep. I toss and turn for an hour before dozing off again.

The wind is starting to pick up again when I awake. It's still dark. I feel disoriented. A distant rumbling grows closer. On the western horizon flames are clearly visible in the darkness but still far away. What's that noise? To the north I see a light, two of them. That's where the sound is coming from. Those are headlights, coming this way.

I can't imagine why anyone would be driving around in this country in the daylight, let alone in the middle of the night. I've been walking a faded jeep trail but haven't seen anyone for a couple days. The lights are getting closer. I'm curious, but not curious enough to get up and walk over to the track. They'll not see me off here. I'll just watch as they go by.

The lights materialize along with the dark form of a truck, slowly grinding along on the rough two-track. They pass me, then stop. There's no way they could see this little tent out here in the dark. The truck starts to back up. Right in front of me, it stops. A spotlight comes on and scans the sagebrush. My pack is lit up. That's what grabbed their interest. A minute ticks by. The light stays on the pack.

"How's it going?" I call out.

I can see the spotlight jump. It flashes over to me and stops. I'm squinting into the blinding light.

"Good God! What on earth are you doing out here?" a voice, excited and curious.

I explain that I'm walking the length of Idaho. They turn the light out of my face. The pack had caught their eye. Even with the spotlight on, they couldn't figure out what it was. It had kind of spooked them. My greeting, a voice from the dark, had made all five of the guys in the truck jump out of their skins.

"They" are BLM firefighters, on their way to fight the grass fire. After a few questions they warn me to keep an eye on it, wish me good luck, and bounce off into the night.

The wind is blowing good now. I can't get back to sleep. The sheep I count turn to roasted lamb. The fire is bothering me. It seems the smoke is worse. Several times I stick my head out to check the western horizon. No use sleeping. The fire is coming my way. I'd better move.

Still weary, but now wide awake, I pack up and start walking north. Night walking always feels a bit surreal. Now, with the haze of the smoke, the distant fires, and the even farther lightning, the entire experience is like a dream. I've slipped into a twilight zone somewhere between heaven and hell. It's beautiful, but in a way I've never seen.

The miles slip by. I'm exhausted, running on empty, stepping like a zombie. The eastern horizon begins to lighten. Fires on both sides of me now. I keep walking. My mind is too weary to realize the sun is coming up.

It feels good to be back at camp. We're hungry, and we rush to fix dinner. These two are good company. I had hoped we'd be able to sit around and swap some songs tonight, but a storm blows in after we're finished eating. We take to our shelters, rain pounding down, water flowing in little rivulets everywhere.

Water. My body craves it. I'm drinking too much and still not getting enough. The air is hot and heavy with the haze of the now-distant fire. My thirst is unquenchable. My water, which should have lasted me a few days, is more than half gone. It's the day after the storm.

This morning I'd slept. Not long, but enough to keep me going. I'd curled up at the base of my pack, too tired to even bother pulling out the sleeping bag. The sun, warming to a burn, had awakened me. It wouldn't let me lie there for long. I got moving again, searching for some shade.

All morning I've walked, drinking from my shrinking supply of water. The heat is intense, especially on the lava. The black rock radiates like a stove. No shade in sight.

By the middle of the afternoon I realize my water is not going to last. The map shows a well a few miles to the east of my route. It's a chance. There may be water. When I come to a jeep trail heading east, I follow it.

The miles are getting longer; at least, they take longer to walk. But I finally see an old stone building, and then a couple weathered outbuildings. It looks like the scene from an old western movie. A dilapidated windmill stands creaking in the breeze. I rush to the well. It's bone dry.

It's pouring. We're feeling snug and dry in the nestlike tent, wondering how Biff is doing under his tarp. The bags are zipped together, and Leslie and I are wrapped in each other's arms, listening to the steady patter of the rain. At this moment I can't imagine wanting to be anywhere else. If only this night could be longer. If only I could stay awake to savor this cozy love we've nestled ourselves in.

I've got to move. When I sit up, the world spins and twirls. I lie back down, not feeling too good. I've been sleeping off the afternoon in one of the creaky old buildings, sheltered from the sun. Rolling over, I stare at my water bottle. The water line is but an inch or two from the bottom. My glances dart away but keep turning back to study this precious thing, as if staring at it will somehow increase its amount. This is getting serious.

It's late afternoon before I get going. Feeling nauseated. Hot. Dry. Weak. Aching legs carry me along. The smoke in the air is oppressive. Each step kicks up a tiny cloud of dust, adding to the haze. I'm on autopilot. The plain is alive around me, and I'm only vaguely aware of it. A badger stares at this waddling stranger. Antelope by the dozen race off when I stagger by. Somewhere birds are singing. I imagine a chorus line of vultures dancing with knives and forks all around me. It's getting dark.

When I lie down for the night, my nausea worsens. My sleep is interrupted with spells of vomiting. This is no way to get rest. As the black of night begins to turn gray, I crawl into the sage one more time and notice the ground is shaking. An earthquake, or me? I'll never know.

I'm walking hard before the sun. Trying to put in miles before the searing heat kicks in. Trying to make way while I can. It's cool now. I hardly notice. The puking is still slowing me down. Costing me precious moisture, too.

Hours later, I'm still teetering along. My strength is gone. My water, too. I'm stopping every quarter mile to either puke or rest. The heat has crazed me. I'm thinking of swimming pools full of iced tea. My body has given up, but for my legs. They have a will of their own. Some distant appointment that must be kept. Some unknown destination they work for. They bear this weary, thirsting body along with no thought, just step after step after step.

The jeep trail has become a little dirt road. Somewhere ahead of me in the glare of the afternoon, a dust cloud emerges. What I think to be a whirlwind is a weathered green pickup truck. I'm staring at it, blankly, when it pulls to a halt next to me. A lady is smiling. "You seen any cows out this way?"

My mouth is so dry, I have trouble talking. "No." It's a big effort to get that one word out. She asks what I'm doing. I offer a raspy answer, telling her. But not everything. I don't tell her about the fire and the dry well. About being so dry I'm sick. Or about the smoke and the heat and the wondering if I was going to make it or not.

She's a rancher. She's a tough, work-hardened, weathered sort. She's staring at me. Hard. Finally, she asks, "Well, do you want a lift? Arco's only fifteen miles. It'd be no trouble for me."

It'd be so easy. No trouble for me either. It's still hard for me to talk. I croak instead of speak my words. Each one is searched out, dredged up, worked hard for. My answer is a ragged whisper. "No thanks. But do you happen to have any water?"

It's raining lightly on the Great Divide. We've just broken from the shelter of the trees and we stop to put on our rain gear. No telling if it'll get worse or not. It doesn't. In fact, as we level off above 9,000 feet, the skies clear and we can see for hundreds of square miles—all the views from yesterday and the distant Italian Peaks and Lemhi Range far to the west.

The distant views are wonderful, but even more interesting are the mountains themselves. The north side of the range drops off in sheer cliffs, sweeping washes, and jagged fins of rock. These steep drops pull at a person to look in, to get as close to the edge as possible to peer over. What is it? The danger? The testing of limits? The walking of that fine line between what is safe and what is death defying? Or is it just something in that gaping space itself? Some magnetism that draws something in our spirit?

Whatever it is, we feel it this day. Time and time again we stop to pause on the edge, gazing into the yawning abyss. The rock itself becomes our focus. We're picking up stones and showing them to each other, a fossil here, a piece of unusual conglomerate there. I'm totally absorbed in the earth at my feet when Biff gasps. Both he and Leslie are staring at the cliff face behind me. Spray-painted in ugly red letters is "Jim Roberts 1972."

We're hurt by this display of vandalism. I wonder aloud if we should add something to this epitaph. Perhaps something appropriate like "is a jerk." Our outrage is replaced by puzzlement. How could this be? How could this remote spot be defaced? What bimbo would carry a can of spray paint in his backpack or saddlebags?

Our answer comes as we continue around the knob and find the south face of the ridge laced with mining roads. The slope has been bulldozed and scraped and dug, apparently with no successful results. But why haven't these roads been reclaimed after the exploratory digging? We've witnessed another abuse that is fairly widespread on our public lands.

After lunch in a wooded pass, we climb back above the trees. A storm is blowing in from the southwest. I'm walking fast. It feels good to be cruising like this. The breeze is cool and the air, charged. I'm charged! My feet feel light, and my legs pump me over the ground like an antelope.

The first crack of thunder, close by, is like a slap in the face. Wake up. This could be dangerous up here. I stop and look around for the others. No one in sight. Great! We should be getting off this ridge, but not before everyone knows where we're going. Another flash of lightning streaks the sky nearby. The thunder shakes the mountain. Leslie appears, walking fast. Her eyes are big. Over the sound of the storm she shouts, "Let's get off the ridge!"

"But Biff won't know where we are. Where is he?"

"I thought he was with you!"

"No, he's still behind somewhere."

"He'd better get here soon. We shouldn't be standing around up here like this."

We wait for what seems like several minutes as the lightning gets closer, the thunder shaking our very bones. Leslie wants to descend. I don't want to leave Biff up here. We start to backtrack, calling his name, both of us worried. Where is he?

"Hi, you guys! What's up?" It's Biff at his best. Totally unconcerned about the storm. We can't be mad. He's so laid back, so mellow, as if it's totally acceptable to walk along an open ridge through the lightning. He's been poking along enjoying the show. His manner is all innocence, and I suppose that's why we love him.

Dropping into a little basin on the Idaho side we weather the storm and set up camp. It's been an excellent day, but we're all tired and ready for the sleeping bags. After dinner, as I'm slipping off to sleep, my last thoughts are to wonder if Biff realized the danger we were in, or if he just enjoyed it. I never asked him.

All Along the Great Divide

You get up in the morning, shake the dew off of
*   your mind,*
As the sun pours like honey through the ponderosa
*   pine,*
You're living every moment as if you've just
*   arrived,*
Because you know what it means to be alive.
*   —from the song "All Along the Great Divide"*

The morning is clear, and when we break camp it's to regain the divide and walk its crest. The views come and go. Our conversation is light. Mostly we walk in our own thoughts, enjoying the quiet and stillness of the mountains.

A couple miles brings us to another pass and a jeep trail that will lead Leslie and Biff back down to the truck several miles away. We stop for a few pictures and a couple heartfelt farewells. I hate to see them go. It'll be a month before I see them again. With a hug and a wave,

Biff starts off down the slope. Leslie lingers, squeezing me tight. These hugs feel good. I hold her to me until she gasps, trying to soak up enough of her to last the next few hundred miles. She goes to leave, but I won't let her. Her tears wet my shirt. Mine make little streaks down my cheeks. The minutes roll by. She turns away, hoists her pack, and is gone.

There's a faded jeep track along the crest. I walk it, sluggishly. Les and Biff are still visible across a wide valley. I'm stopping every hundred yards to watch them. For a mile we wave across the widening distance. The last I see them, they're tiny dots disappearing into a break in the forest. I'm alone again. The mountains suddenly feel much wilder, a touch more free.

This is a curious phenomenon. I am a human, yet when I walk alone, I feel less allegiance to my own species, and more to the entire world around me. As much as I love Leslie, my friends, and people in general, their presence blocks something from me. To go with others is to have a good time and feel and see things, but all through a human's eyes, as part of the herd. When I'm walking with others I listen to the wild, but I'm also listening to what we're saying as we chat our miles away. Conversation is fun and it is wonderful, but it is not walking softly. It is not being in touch with what's going on around us. Conversation keeps the wilderness at bay. Company is a security blanket that insulates us from the world we wander through. To go alone is to truly experience wilderness.

The aloneness I feel today is a good aloneness. It is not loneliness. This aloneness soothes and welcomes. It is a feeling of being in balance and in tune. The solitude wilderness can offer is perhaps one of its greatest assets to today's humans. Being alone is a rare thing in our ever-crowded society. Being alone with nature is even more rare. That scarcity alone makes it precious, but it becomes priceless when we add the experience of tranquil communion with our living planet. The chance to cut distractions and focus on our connections with the Earth, with God, and with our selves is a gift of the wild country, a blessing I feel honored to receive.

My route drops me slightly into the basin of Odell Creek. It's a peaceful place. The tiny stream meanders quietly through flowered meadows and scattered patches of trees. It's good to walk such a place. The critters like it, too: lots of elk sign, and farther upstream, several beaver dams with a lodge.

I spend an hour poking through the meadows, then climb quickly back to the crest of the forested Continental Divide. Here is something I recall from my Mexico-to-Canada hike eleven years ago: a massive, aged Douglas fir, its bark gnarled and weathered from centuries of clinging to the crest of the continent. Immediately I dub it "Centennial Tree."

Centennial Tree is one of those trees you just can't pass by without stopping to touch. I try. Oh, I do stop and stare at it from the trail a few long minutes, but then I walk on, only to halt twenty yards later and glance back. The glance is what does it. I lower my pack and walk back to the base of the giant old monarch. The rugged bark feels good to my hands. The deep furrows and wrinkled contours demand a caress here, a gentle touch there. Without thinking, my arms reach out. They stretch but a tiny way around the ancient trunk, but it's an embrace of respect and love. I step away from the elder and return to my pack. It sounds corny, I know, but I feel much better. Now I can move on.

When I last walked this stretch of the range, I stayed with the divide, making my way along the trackless crest and using snowmelt for my water. Today I've decided to go a different way and drop down to Aldous Lake. I don't remember this trail being here in the seventies. Nor is it shown on the map I have now. The path crosses the crest and turns south, not the way I want to be going. After leaving the trail, I make my way easily down the steep wooded slope. The big trees are widely scattered, and it's a good route down.

Just when the tilt of the slope and the steady downhill jarring are starting to get to me, the steepness slackens. I come upon a tiny hidden glade tucked amid immense Douglas and subalpine fir. A spring gushes from the mountain a few yards above me, pouring its pure icy water over a carpet of mossy green rocks. The verdant color radiates along that ribbon of bubbling water, and with it, a fresh earthy scent of damp turf, tangy sap, and soaked rocks. A small patch of flat ground carpeted with a dense layer of fir needles welcomes me to sit a spell.

Paradise is an overused, tired kind of word. (You found paradise? That's niiice.) But at this moment, I've stumbled upon it. I lie upon the forest floor in this perfect place. The trees arching overhead form a cozy cathedral-like niche. The spring murmurs, singing a gentle sonata, easing me toward a euphoric peace.

I could stay here forever, slipping into a timeless void. I'd live off the cool spring waters, lying like a log on this spot, still and silent. Rabbits would nestle against my warmth. Birds would nest in my tangled hair. Bear and elk would step over me as they came and went. The fairies and wood nymphs would dance around me by the light of the full moon. It would be a good life, a studious life, for I would not just be lying about like a bum. No, I would be there to study this place. I'd be working. I'd be listening to the lectures of time, studying the silence of the forest and the peace of the quiet. I'd be researching the fall of fir needles, the song of the spring, the effects of dancing sprites on the forest ecosystem. Serious stuff, but somebody has to do it.

The water songs lull me to sleep. When I awake, I sit up with a start, having no idea how long it's been. What day is this? What century? If Rip Van Winkle slept for twenty years, could I have missed ten or fifteen? But there are no needles piled upon me. My hair and beard are still dark and fairly short. I lie back against my pack. Still too soon to push on.

This place brings me dreams. Awake now but not totally conscious in all respects, I let my thoughts flitter here and there from the trees to the spring, to the vibrant life all about me. The wilderness is full of such down-to-earth pleasures.

I was always a bit in awe of my great grandmother Grandma Bee, who first encouraged me to appreciate the treasures of the wild. When I was ten years old she led me into her room at my Grandma Jessie's to present me with a special gift. Totally absorbed in her every word and move, I watched with growing interest as she lifted a foot-long, shallow box from the dresser and placed it in my hands.

I think it must have been a box for some kind of jewelry. It was strong finished cardboard with a reddish brown glaze. It had an old smell, musty, like Grandma Bee's room. When I carefully lifted the lid, I beheld a carpet of cotton batting cradling a sea of treasures. She explained each one to me as I examined them: two perfectly flat, oval petosky stones (a local fossil found on the beaches of northwestern Michigan), a piece of British soldier (a red-capped lichen), a pine cone, a bit of gray lichen, a tiny tooth from some kind of rodent, the jawbone of the same rodent, and the most precious thing, a swallowtail butterfly, wings outspread, dead and dry but oh so beautiful.

Grandma Bee said she thought I needed a treasure box. She knew I would value these objects. I don't think she ever knew just how much I would. For years I would cherish the moment of opening that little box. I would add more riches to it. I would grow into, and learn more about, the wondrous world of the outdoors the box represented. But I would never tire of beholding those simple gifts.

I was a boy scout. Not for long, just a few years. I never made it to eagle scout, but I learned a lot in scouting. Not so much about backpacking, but about life. Mr. Bersch was our scout leader. He played a folk guitar and knew dozens of old folk songs. He also knew kids. He had a way about him that made folks feel good when they were with him. He took the scout oath and law seriously. Things like truth and trust, kindness and courage were things to put into action, to live by. I wanted to be like him. When I look back through all these years, I realize he, too, gave me a treasure box full of riches, bits of wisdom to live with. More simple gifts.

My life has had its hard times, the sour, mean, and ugly times. But my life has also had those precious sprinklings of inspiration that have pointed me in the direction I walk today. Simple gifts I've been allowed to see for what they truly are, power points in a growing life.

There was the time I ran away from home fully intending to live off what I could catch with my fishing pole, returning hours later with the excuse that I'd forgotten the bait. The real reason I came back was for love of family. Swimming with Mom and Dad, holding on to them, scared, but knowing they wouldn't let me go. Ever. The times sailing with Dad on the most perfect summer days, riding before the wind, floating for miles down the lake, loving him. Diving for sunken treasure, golf balls and lost anchors, with Mark and my cousins Bob and Rick, being a part of a larger family. Ringing the big brass bell in front of my grandparents' house and hearing the sweet tones echoing across Torch Lake, wishing I could travel with the sound waves, an endless rippling adventure. And Mom, watching my youngest sister, Lisa, graduate from college, the only one of her four kids to do so. The look of pride on her face, the tears in her eyes, bring a dampness to mine.

Simple gifts, but gifts nonetheless. A lifetime of orienting and learning, and not always realizing the lesson until sometimes years later.

This hidden spring and a thousand others have blessed me. They pile up in my memories like building blocks forming a foundation of love that ties me to the god dwelling in each and every thing. That bond with the One strengthens me, fills me up, and lightens me. It connects me not only to the planet but to the universe. And with that spiritual connection comes the gift of warm security, a sense of home wherever I wander, a sense of who I am and where I fit into that home.

The gifts of the wild are not always tangible. They are often unclaimed moods or feelings gained from time with nature. A sweet contentment often walks with me when I'm out here, a flowing peace of mind. Perhaps this is why I often describe wilderness as a state of mind. Nature is always there, but our attitude, and how we relate to nature, often determines how we behold it. Our experience with the wild country, and what we derive from it, is directly related to this. More gifts are served up on the plate of the natural world, on the solitude of the place and the time.

The song of the spring suddenly increases in volume. I roll on my side to study it. It doesn't seem to be flowing any more than it was a moment ago. Why should it suddenly sound louder? As I listen, it does change volume. In fact, the bubbling song changes constantly, weaving a gentle cloak of sound, engulfing me. I'm staring at the little sliver of water, but I'm not conscious of seeing it. My ears are all that's working. Sound is the only thing getting through to my brain. Once there, it's not bouncing off thought but rather soaking into some far corner—a sound dream.

Later, I hoist the pack. It's time to move on. Looking over the mossy spring once more, I wonder, have I stumbled upon the most beautiful place on Earth? I think perhaps I have, for today. The view also depends upon what thoughts accompany the sight. My sweet memories of youth have also sweetened this spring water. I give a soft, "Thank you," and walk away.

I'm feeling good, as content as I ever will be, as aware as my conscious self will know. Surely this day is blessed. Walking through this old-growth forest is a thanksgiving. But suddenly the forest ends.

The perfect forest has given way to huge stumps and piles of old slash. I step over a pile of debris to a giant stump and step up onto the wide platform to survey the old cut. True, it isn't as bad as some I've seen. Some trees were left standing. But there is a feeling of tilt here. Having just experienced what the majestic climax forest can offer, I mourn the passing of what must have thrived here.

The stump itself is what saddens me most. I can gaze out over the slash and weed-cloaked ruins of a forest, but my focus comes back to the gray, sun-bleached remains of this particular tree. Here, the loss becomes personalized. How high had this giant stood? Judging by its width it must have towered over this canyon. I can stretch out across the grain. The stump is at least eight feet in diameter. How old was this monarch? The circling lines of age are weathered and worn, impossible to read. Several centuries is a good guess.

It's like visiting an old graveyard and wondering about the personalities behind the names and dates. What ever happened to the rest of this tree? Where did its sturdy heartwood end up? Who used its strong, true timbers? Did the user ever stop to think about the life, or the history, they borrowed?

Did those fine timbers build a happy home? Or a piece of lovely furniture? An instrument of song? I pray it was something done with pride, something done to last. Not some tacky tract home or useless bit of froufrou. Life deserves more than that. How good life would be if we could all be more conscious of where things come from, if we could turn away from blind consumption and live with more awareness of the life around us.

I jump off the massive stump and make my way slowly through the cut, back into a living forest. The trail to Aldous Lake is easy to find. It's a real showcase of a trail. A lot of thought was put into it. The grade is easy, with lots of water bars and tiny bridges over wet spots. Good job. It leads me through a mature forest. I love it. I really do. I just can't shake the ghost of the big stump. I can't shake the ghosts of a thousand stumps, the millions of stumps appearing everywhere across the West.

Yes, I know logging is a necessary activity. As the corporate leaders ask, "You use toilet paper don't you?" As if that has anything to do with the issue. Do we have to stand for overcutting our native forests and denuding our sensitive high-elevation forests because we are consumers? I don't think so.

The fact is that our national forest system is being run into the ground. Forests that could be providing a stable, sustainable economy to western communities for centuries down the road will instead simply be gone. Boom and bust. Use it up and move on when it's gone. That's how we still operate in this enlightened age. U.S. taxpayers are subsidizing the destruction by continuing to build roads for below-cost timber sales and by turning a blind eye to the degradation of the public lands.

I happen to believe that logging is a respectable occupation. It is something that I know can be done with respect to the forest and sensitivity to the life that abounds there. Instead of logging in half-mile wide swaths of destruction, where nearly every tree is cut down and so many just laid to waste, selective cutting needs to be instituted. Cut the trees that are crowding out others. Cut only the trees that will be used. Cut a variety of species and ages, leaving a diverse forest. Use horses or light machines and minimal roads. Leave the riparian areas intact. No cutting close to streams. Respect and care need to go hand in hand when it comes to modern logging. Unfortunately, I rarely see it being done in such a manner.

I'm walking fast now. The path is perfect for stepping out. The harder the questions, the faster my pace, but I've learned long ago that no one can outwalk these things. The wild country will recharge you, but walk far enough and eventually you will come to another clear-cut, another road, another subdivision. I walk toward it as I walk away from it, for in seeking out the last wild places, in attempting to understand and celebrate them, I also must understand the wave of humanity that eats away at the wildland's borders with more ferocity each passing year. I must come face to face with the monster that gobbles up everything in its path. It is myself. It is you. It is all of us.

Aldous Lake is a tiny lake. I drop my pack and walk around it in fifteen minutes. There's a nice campground on the west side, and I set up my camp there, doing laundry, oiling my boots, swimming in the lake, and generally enjoying the sunny afternoon. After dinner the warmth of the sun vanishes in minutes. A mountain storm punches its way across the range, bringing thunder and lightning with waves of downpours. I fall into a sound sleep, lulled by the patter of unending rain.

The pelting rain is still with me when I awake. No sense rushing into things. I watch the morning creep into day from the comfort of my bag. Time to pull out a book, write a few letters, scribble some lines of poetry.

Aldous Lake

Thunder rolls on the plains below,
A distant call to awaken rain and wind.
Here, nested upon the mountain's arm,
The lake holds on . . .
In stillness.
Clouds drag heavily, drooping at peace,
Settling in to worship rusted calm.

The insides of clouds differ from their outer shell.
Gone are the lines of distinction and mobility,
The proud chin, the thrusting forehead,
The fierce massive.
Instead, the heart is wispy and soft,
Spread thin to coat each new bone within its grasp.
Cloaked gray to mesh the silence
With the sound of its own dripping soul,
The touch of rain,
A whisper through the forest,
Comes chasing the dawn.

It's midday before I pack up and leave the lake. The showers have ceased. The day is cool and overcast. I've been feeling lazy all morning, but once I'm up and walking I feel strong. Really strong. Like I can hike to the moon and back.

The miles fly by. On gray days like this it's hard to judge my progress, either in miles or time of day. A dull sameness hangs over the range with the dense mat of clouds. I enjoy days like this. The moist air lends vitality and freshness to the mountains, soaking into every pore of every being. Drops of the passing rain hang on the tip of each minute needle of fir, each blade of bent grass, every wispy fern.

Certain colors seem much more vibrant on such days. Greens never look so green. Today the living colors jump out like neon; they fairly glow in places with a spectrum of shades for every bend in the trail. The day is uneventful in terms of major adventures; but for pure joy of hiking, the magic factor rides high.

Salamander Lake, a shallow pond below the divide, is an unappealing place on this cloudy day, but I stop in a stand of fir there and make camp. No sign of any salamanders in the pond but much evidence of elk and coyote. After dinner the sun peeks through for a few moments. It looks like a giant eye peering down at me through the curtain of clouds. With a wink, it's gone.

This morning I'm excited to get going. I bounce out of the bag at first light, pack the tent while eating breakfast, and am soon walking up the trail. The air is cool, the ground wet. My steps are soft. The clouds begin to lift and the sun pours in. Just as I crest the divide again, an old bull moose spooks from his breakfast spot and lopes away, long legs stiff and straight like a ballerina, covering ground.

An old trail runs along the ridge, little used with lots of blow-downs. It's an excellent walk. I get occasional views to the north, and wind through healthy stands of fir and whitebark pine. A large herd of elk, mostly cows, is roused. Their mews and calls blend with the distant cry of a red-tailed hawk. Lots of hawks today.

After climbing a very narrow point in the ridge, I can hear the bleating of hundreds of sheep. Sounds like a big flock. A quarter mile later I pass above the main bunch, a mass of jostling bodies. Up higher, where I stride, a few small bands scatter as I approach. The earth is pawed and nibbled, droppings everywhere.

I like seeing sheep. They don't bother me as much as cows do. Sheep have some esthetics, some pastoral color to their presence. I know that sheep tend to eat a wider variety of plant life than cows do, but I don't know which has more impact. I tend to think that cows do just because they'll stay in one spot for weeks totally trashing an area, while the sheep have a herder whose job it is to keep them on the move.

There are many facets to this grazing issue: the loss of wildlife habitat, soil erosion, degradation of water quality, social and economic impacts on the ranching communities, loss of biodiversity, extinction of salmon and various other species, and the one that raises my hackles in an instant—the practice of predator control. This year the federal government will spend approximately $17,000,000 killing wildlife through its Animal Damage Control (ADC) program. The ADC not only kills so-called "problem" animals (those that get in the way of human development and livestock), but indiscriminately goes after any predator having the misfortune to be in the hunted area. Predators are killed just because they are predators.

The ADC kills thousands and thousands of animals, often doing away with other species that accidentally get into the traps or poison. The waste of wild lives, dollars, and energy is obvious. The sad part is that viable alternatives are available. Special guard dogs, llamas, and even donkeys raised with the herd are finding much success in deterring predators. Having a herdsperson with the livestock is a sure way to keep predators away. Keeping the animals moving and out of high risk areas is also an obvious answer, but often totally overlooked. We don't need to be killing off all these animals. Recent studies have shown that control (killing) of coyotes often increases the conflict with ranchers. Older, wiser animals who may learn to stay away from people and their livestock are replaced by young, untested coyotes who find it easier to kill a calf or a lamb.

The sheep are a couple miles behind me now as I arrive at Rock Spring. A herder's camp is set up around the spring. A few horses eye me warily as I approach. I'm watching for the dogs. There's got to be dogs. There always is, ornery ones too. Perhaps if I step lightly enough they won't see me. No such luck. One dog spots me and sounds the alarm. Immediately three mongrels are on the attack.

1975—WESTERN NEW YORK STATE

The bulldog appears out of nowhere, growling and snapping like a bear. The walking stick keeps him at bay at first. I point it and shake it at him, and he backs off. I'm glancing up at the farmhouse I was walking past, hoping the dog's owner will call the dog off.

The snarling dog dodges around the stick. I whack him over the head. He tries again. I clobber him good.

Finally a voice from the house assures me, "Oh, that's Snapper. He won't bite!"

Tell Snapper that, mister.

The dogs are having a wild time of it, barking and growling. This is exciting stuff for them. Something's invading and they've got to protect their home turf. They circle me like pros, dodging behind me to try and nip my legs. I'm watching closely, flailing about with my walking stick, trying to keep them off, when the herder comes out from the tent to join me. He curses the dogs by name and grabs whatever is handy to throw at them; sticks, rocks, a canteen, coffee pot, and so on. He's reaching for a coil of rope when the last of the dogs creeps away, tail between its legs.

The man is a thin, wiry kind of guy. He looks about sixty, but it's hard to tell. He's been in the sun a lot, tan and wrinkled. He walks stiffly, like it's a chore. Once the dogs are under control (he throws something at them every couple minutes just for good measure), we settle into a nice conversation.

Over the years I've met many sheepherders. They're almost always friendly, even the ones who can't speak English. I've always admired the solitary lifestyle of these men. Often their little gypsy-like wagon is hauled in ahead of time and they are packed into the wagon site by horses with their supplies and gear. The herders don't see many folks during their summer in the high country. Keeping tabs on the herd, they move them from meadow to meadow, always on the go, always aware of what's going on in the mountains around them. But like the wild mountains themselves, they are becoming a rare and endangered breed. The price of wool lingers at record lows, and many sheep owners find it more profitable to keep the herd out of the high country. Good for the wild places, but not for the herders.

West of Rock Spring I cross a series of broad meadows and then several miles of relatively flat, forested ridge. I'm watching for a section of trail I know I will recognize from my 1979 Mexico-to-Canada hike.

1979—CENTENNIAL MOUNTAINS, IDAHO/MONTANA

This is just the right kind of trail for making time. Not overly worn, the ground is soft, with some give to it. It feels good on my feet. I'm in high gear, stepping out. The past few miles have been relatively flat along this gentle ridge. Now I'm starting to climb. I've drifted into a void as I puff up the slope. Lungs chugging, legs pounding, I've sealed out the world around me. The motion of muscle and the few feet of path before me are my entire world—until I hear something move.

The noise isn't loud. Just enough to brush my consciousness, enough to make me glance up the trail. A large black bear is rising up on its hind legs. As she rears up, she woofs out a warning. I halt in surprise as a cub scurries up a tree behind Mama, whimpering like a baby.

"Geez!" The sow is staring down at me, towering like a mountain. I back down the trail, unbuckling my pack. Turning away, I walk with one eye over my shoulder. Mama bear watches me solemnly until I'm out of sight.

Today as I walk this stretch of trail there are no bears. I can picture Mama Bear standing right about here. I look down the path to where I had stood gaping up at her. I remember being scared. I remember being thrilled. The image of the big bear towering over me is easy to bring back. What I can't recall is the sweat in my armpits, the vulnerability, the uncertainty that came with the fear. I know those things must have been there. I know I was afraid. Today I grope for those lost sensations, but they're too far back. Too many miles and bends in the trail have faded their tracks.

I love this range. Foot travel is easy. The views are wonderful. The trees are big and healthy. But when I really think about my time in this wilderness, or for that matter my time in any wild country, the encounters and experiences with wildlife are what make up most of my special wilderness memories. Wild lives make the wild country what it is.

We humans are herd animals. We need companionship. We seek it out, and not just with our own species. Our hearts brighten with the sighting of each new creature we meet. A land can't be lonely when other life flourishes there. What a lonesome place this Earth would be without our fellow creatures.

My memories of various mountain ranges inevitably tie directly with wildlife encountered in those places. The Ruby Range of Nevada: a junco landing on my shoulder. The Olympic Peninsula: a herd of Roosevelt elk racing over a ridge and into a sun setting into my first glimpse of the Pacific Ocean. The Boulder Range of Idaho: a mountain goat showing me a route over the crest. The Santa Rita Mountains of Arizona: tracking a lion for miles through waste-deep snow. The Centennials will always conjure up Mama Bear. These are bits of magic woven forever into the fabric of my life. It is a blessing to share this wonderful planet with all the life that can abound here. Yet each year at least 20,000 species go extinct due to human maltreatment of the environment. Have we lost touch so much? With each species the Earth loses, we lose, too, a part of ourselves, a part of our own connection to this lovely Earth, a part of our own roots.

The Pete Creek Divide is a low, wooded pass on the crest of the Continental Divide. I slept here in '79 under a big Doug fir. Today, under that same tree, I take a break and munch some trail mix. I'll need the fuel on the big climb up to Little Table Mountain.

After lunch, the climb doesn't seem as steep as I remembered it. In no time I'm leveling out on the broad, open crest. The forest has given way to vast meadows and wide panoramas. The narrow footpath becomes a rutted jeep trail. Storm clouds are brewing all about me. The wind is whipping and tugging at my pack. My heart is as big as the view. I'm singing.

All along the Great Divide, yes, we can understand,
What it means to be alive, all along the Great Divide.

The song "All Along the Great Divide" is one of the most popular songs I sing. It started right here. Originally written " a man can understand" from my own perspective, my first recording of it has it this way, but since '89 when Leslie walked the Colorado portion of the Continental Divide with me, I've sung it "we can understand." It's no longer just my song. It's our song.

The song began here and was finished more than a month later in Glacier National Park. I alternate between singing and humming it to myself as I walk against the fierce wind. A couple miles later the rumbling of thunder tells me it's time to call it a day. At a low point in the ridge I drop back into the forest toward the sound of falling water.

~

Gone are the blasts of thunder, the flashes of lightning; likewise the fierce pounding of hail and rain. I think the stillness of this morning is what awakens me. The sudden calm reclaiming the day prods me to consciousness. The only sounds are the tiny creek in the gorge below me, and the slow dripping of the remnants of last night's storm.

I feel satisfied. Content. Last night I wrote a new song, a humorous look at the food chain. Today is a town day for me. My first of this trek. I will hike a dozen miles to Interstate 15 and hitch a ride to the nearest town, Lima, for supplies, phone calls, a hot shower, and a night under a roof. Maybe a few treats, too. More than anything, I'm anxious to call Mom and Leslie. Better get going.

When I climb up onto the open crest again, the skies to the east still hold a dense blanket of fog. The air feels heavy with moisture. The scent of the soaked meadows, the dense grass, permeates the morning. My boots are soon soaked from plodding across the wet turf. A couple miles later the sun begins to burn the clouds away. Antelope race over the rolling hills. Hawks swoop overhead. I come upon a pair of sandhill cranes with a young one (called a colt). The parents attempt to draw me away, one of them feigning an injury. I let them lead me. Their distant calls, ringing like ancient voices, are all the reward I need.

Several hours of walking brings me to a point where I leave the divide and the faint trace of a trail. The last mile to the tiny village of Monida, Montana, is down open grass-covered slopes. When I step onto the county road, my socks look as if they were a coat of fur, the seeds from the grass are so densely imbedded.

Monida was one of Montana's first tourist towns. In the 1800s, it was the gateway to Yellowstone National Park. Folks would take the train as far as Monida, then board stagecoaches for the long ride through the Centennial Valley and east to the park. At one time Monida was a happening place with a hotel and post office and many stores.

Today it's quiet. Several houses and numerous empty, boarded-up buildings make up the village. This is my third time to walk through Monida. It's become a landmark for me. I like it. The few houses are neat and well cared for. The abandoned businesses, some with false fronts, lend it a historical mood. I remember it as a friendly place, folks waving and smiling to a traveling stranger, little encounters that make being a human so special.

1976—Skagit River Valley, Washington

The little dirt road I've been walking all day is leading me past an old farmhouse. The trim little building is nearly buried under a forest of well-tended shrubs and trees. The fenced yard is overflowing in color, flowers in full bloom splashed into every nook and cranny. The garden is a paradise, but the lady in the middle of it is what really catches my eye. She's an elderly woman, bent and frail, with gray hair pulled back tightly, draped over her shoulder. She stands in the middle of the flowers, a solemn island, gazing poignantly at the plant life surrounding her, looking like Mother Nature herself. As I draw closer, she catches the movement on the road and looks up. I wave. She waves back. Somehow we start talking, and I wander over to the fence.

Something about this woman draws me. She must be in her seventies. I'm only twenty-three. Yet, some bond here, some common thread ties two strangers together. Sometimes it's easier to talk to someone you don't know, to share details that might be lost to others. In minutes, we are sharing an intimate conversation, baring our souls over the fence.

She and her husband have lived here for over forty years. They built the place. They raised children (and flowers) over those years. Their home has been the perfect home, a place of warmth and love. She loves the place, especially this garden and her lovely flowers. Listening to her, I feel the lively color must symbolize her entire life.

Her husband has been ill as of late. He can't get around. She's having trouble caring for him on her own. In a few weeks they'll be leaving the place, moving into town. Her voice has a catch in it when she mentions leaving. She looks long and wistfully at the flowers.

We talk for a long time. I've taken off the pack and am leaning on the fence with both arms. I tell her about my life. She shares hers. I feel like the thousands of miles I've walked are but a splash next to her life with her loving family. At last it's time for me to move on. I hoist the pack and shake her hand. We say our good-byes, and I turn to the road. I've taken a dozen steps when she shouts after me, "You know?"

I stop and turn. "What?" I ask.

"Isn't it nice to run into a friend once in a while?"

Yes, I think it is.

Monida is not so friendly today. In fact, it's almost hostile. The first person I see is an old man. I wave and say hello. Without acknowledging me, he turns away. The next two people give me the same cold shoulder. It's as if I'm not even there. What happened to the friendly place I'd known before? Is this a sign of the times?

Interstate 15 isn't your typical expressway. Yes, it does look like the average interstate, but the amount of traffic is considerably less than on most highways. I walk up the entrance ramp and plunk down the pack, confident of catching a ride for the fourteen miles into Lima. My confidence fades with the hours.

I don't like hitchhiking, at least not with my big pack. Years ago I used to travel quite a bit on my thumb. It was cheap, easy, and relatively safe. On my long walks, I've often hitched into a town for supplies and then back to the trail to resume the trek. But more than anything else, getting into that car breaks the flow of the trip. Perhaps the speed causes this break, or maybe the miles without effort. Whatever it is, I've tried to avoid it as much as possible these last several years. Unfortunately, this is a spot where I must resupply. I wave my thumb at each passing vehicle. No one stops.

I make a sign with a page from my journal. It says "Lima" in big dark letters. I want to write, "I Don't Bite." The occasional cars race on by. It's hot in the sun. My water is nearly gone. I pace up and down the shoulder. I count cars. 12, 13, 14, 15, 16, 17, . . . I think of the fear we Americans live in today. Are we as free as we think we are if we're afraid to talk to a stranger? 29, 30, 31, 32, 33, 34, . . .

At last a railroad man, covered in sweat, dirty and dry as I am, stops and smiles a greeting. In no time, I'm flying along at seventy miles per hour.

Lost Horizons
and Hidden
Valleys

Mountains are more than just piles of stone,
They're alive with a heart all their own.
And the creatures that roam there and live there
*   and die there,*
This, they all seem to know.
                    —from the song "Wild Wind"

It's hot. Not a tree in sight. The sun beats down on the dusty dirt lane and reflects back up at me. I'm sweating buckets. My pack is loaded down with thirteen days of food. I should be wilting. Instead, I'm feeling charged. One night in town and I'm ready to get back into the wild country. I'm stepping out.

Leslie surprised me last night. She showed up in Lima. We had a quiet evening taking showers, cleaning gear, cuddling in bed. Before she arrived, Jack and Kathy Kirkley had stopped by the motel. Jack will be leaving a food drop for me at an abandoned farmhouse in a couple weeks.

I also called Mom. She talked on the phone but didn't sound good. My sister, Lisa, told me that she'd been doing great up until now. Mom said, "I'm just having a bad day."

Leslie drove me back to Monida this morning. We got a late start. It was easier departing this time. She drove away with a kiss on her lips. I walked into Idaho, climbed a fence to cross the freeway, and started back into the mountains.

After I've come six miles since I first hoisted the pack onto my back in Monida, I'm overdue for a break. Ahead of me the first trees appear next to Modoc Creek. When I finally get to the cool shade, I can't get the pack off quickly enough. Yes, that's better. Time to chug a bottle of water and gobble a handful of Leslie's homemade chocolate chip cookies. Most rest stops for me are also a time to get my bearings, pull out the map, renew my sense of where I am. The stretch west of Monida Pass is an area that I've walked twice before. It's an area I should know, yet in my memories it appears only as a vast gray area.

The first time through, I was using a general Forest Service map. Nothing made sense. I couldn't orient the map to what I was experiencing on the ground, so the hike felt disjointed through here. Seven years later I wasn't even using maps. By the last weeks of a 1,700 mile trek from Arizona, three hundred miles from home, I'd thrown away all my maps. It led to many good adventures but didn't make the lay of the land any clearer. Now I've got the topographical maps. I'm going to get a handle on this thing.

This is interesting country, rugged and fairly open. The map has very little green on it. The forests grow in the sheltered canyons and on the north-facing slopes. The ridges are long and narrow, excellent for walking. All I have to do is get up to them.

I turn up the west fork of Modoc. The trail shown on my 1957 map becomes fainter with each quarter mile, gradually disappearing. The slope becomes steeper, my steps slower. I make little switchbacks up the grassy slope, chugging away, inching upward, higher and higher. The views get broader and more expansive. At last the earth levels out and I find myself atop the ridge. The Continental Divide is just to the north of me a couple hundred yards. The skies are clear. The crest route looks inviting.

Several minutes later I'm standing atop the divide again, one foot in Idaho, another in Montana. The wind slaps at me, whipping my shirt and tugging at my beard. This wayward breeze has come a long way to push this sweaty hiker around. Miles of Idaho desert wear its tracks. It's only fitting that it should come seeking the mountain heights after so much time in those lower plains. Like a long lost friend, I welcome this wind rustling my hair and watering my eyes. Not only does it invigorate, but today it inspires. With each gust I become more empowered, as if the wind itself is inflating me with energy. I can see for hundreds of square miles, and now I feel as if I can walk every one of them.

For two miles, I walk the divide, up and down a series of minor knobs. I'm conscious of the crest of the continent today. This spine of Earth, winding and twisting its way through the mountains, intrigues me. I'm constantly drawn to it. Walking the divide, I can feel its continuity, sense those miles, and grasp the immensity of this Earth's mantle. It grants me that sense of smallness that is at once humbling yet also fulfilling. These miles on the Great Divide connect me, not only to myself and my species, but to the very planet itself. I never feel like more of an Earthling, my sense of place assured, than when I walk the Continental Divide.

Later, the skies that have looked so clear begin to turn dark and menacing. My leisurely pace is gone. I'm walking faster, looking for a good place to get off the precipitous ridge. Thunder rumbles, then more thunder, closer this time. A bolt of lightning shoots toward the earth a mile away. The blast of accompanying thunder shakes me and the mountain I'm standing on. Time to get off this exposed ridge. A narrow canyon on the Montana side is handy. I scurry down the rocky slope and find a fairly sheltered spot to take a break. The storm, roaring and flashing, passes over with only a few drops of rain. Twenty minutes later the skies are clear. I hike back up to the crest.

The shadows are getting longer. Time to look for some water and a place to camp. Mill Fork of Middle Creek looks good on the Idaho side. There are some trees down there. The gully is steep. I carefully pick my way down and enter the forest. In the shade the air is cooler. It's very still and quiet here. The wind of the peaks is but a distant memory in this sheltered nook. The trees are giants, an island of old-growth Doug fir. They would be inspiring anywhere, but among the barren slopes, tucked away in these sun-bleached grassy mountains, this hidden grove appears all the more special.

In search of water and a flat spot to sleep, I keep dropping lower into the canyon. Surely there is water down here somewhere. Instead, I find a mule deer fawn, her mother nowhere in sight. She eyes me curiously as I trek by thirty yards away.

Eventually the creek starts flowing. A gnarly Doug fir standing over an oxbow of the tiny stream beacons the perfect place to sleep. The trickle of water is just enough for a pot bath. It's icy and hurts at first, but a bath like this is well worth any nineteen-mile day. Especially today.

Dinner is accompanied by a stunning array of cloud formations. They build up like buckling ice floes, spilling across the heavens, flowing in waves of glory. All the while the setting sun is painting these massive, shifting shapes in hues of pink and violet. The glow of the skies settles over the canyon. I offer a prayer of thanks, a song of celebration. On the mountain to the west of me a coyote does the same.

Through the dull fuzziness of sleep a distant bleating squirms into my consciousness. Over and over again the plaintive cry breaks the morning. I roll onto my stomach and look out the open door of the tent. The crying is louder now, drawing closer. The faint rustle of steps is barely discernible, approaching with the mournful sound.

My view out of the tent is limited, and I'm lying still, waiting. Whatever it is must be within feet of where I lie. Suddenly a tiny head peeks around the edge of my tent. The fawn from yesterday is looking in at me. She sniffs and tilts her head. Her ears twitch. She steps around the corner into full view, looking as if she might come on in.

I'm trying not to breathe or even blink. She gives another cry, like a little lamb, and stares at me. I have to tell myself not to reach out to comfort her. Wouldn't it be nice to stroke that soft fur? She gives another sniff and turns away, looking up the canyon, her back to me. Another cry and she moves on.

The fawn is obviously searching for her mother. I wonder how many days she'll last on her own before she feeds the coyotes. She's a cute little thing, but so are coyote pups. It all works out in the end.

Somewhere along the line, we all feed something else, whether it's other predators or the Earth itself. I don't slight the coyotes their meal, but I have to admit that I wish the fawn had stayed longer with her mother.

It's funny how we relate to predators. In our culture, we learn that there are good animals and bad animals. Deer and elk are good. Wolves and coyotes are not. Why is that? Why is it OK for humans to kill deer but not for coyotes to do the same? Why does modern human, surely the most effective predator on the face of the Earth, cringe at the idea of one animal eating another?

Slowly, we as a people are regaining a more reasonable attitude toward predators, one that accepts the rights of other creatures to exist, one that acknowledges the truths of nature and the cycle of death giving to life. This is knowledge we once lived by, way back when. It is a knowledge that I hope we will live by again.

What would have happened to me if my mother hadn't been around when I was a babe? My father was an orphan. Lots of children are. But at this moment I can't imagine my life without the stalwart presence of that woman, my mother. I couldn't imagine it thirty-seven years ago; I can't imagine it now. Like these mountains I walk, her presence is part of the permanency of my world, a constant that I can always depend on. But I wonder, did the fawn feel as secure in her mother's existence? "I'm just having a bad day." My mother's words to me on the phone. Perhaps.

Sometimes I can conjure up Mom's smile. Or even her angry yell. If I think about it, I can smell her, or feel her big arms around me. Her laugh is easy to bring up. Those are good thoughts. Special feelings. Today, all morning, they roll around and keep coming back.

I'm following the faint trace of a jeep trail up the left fork of Middle Creek. The hillsides are trampled and grazed. Looks like another herd of sheep up here somewhere.

Eventually I can hear the herd. Rounding a bend in the narrow canyon, I find the entire band being driven toward me. A herder on horseback and his two dogs are getting a good workout. I plow through the sheep, and a few scatter up the hill. The dogs are good.

Without a word they're on the deserters, driving them back to the main herd. I like these dogs. They're smooth and know what they're doing. They ignore me. They're having too much fun with the sheep anyway. These dogs belong here. This is what they do best and they obviously enjoy this job. The herder is another story.

He ignores the first wave of greeting. I try again. He nods solemnly. This guy doesn't want to be out here. When I get closer my attempts at conversation are in vain. He's obviously not having a good morning. I'm glad when he rides on. Maybe the dogs will cheer him up.

The trace disappears and the mountainsides close in. I head straight up the slope, grunting back up to the divide. It's a good morning to be on the crest of the continent. Hundreds of square miles are clearly in view, all the way from the ghostly Tetons and the Madison, Gravelly, and Snowcrest Ranges to the Italian Peaks and the Lemhi and Lost River Ranges in Idaho. Three large cinder cones rise above the desert of the Snake River Plain. The divide meanders on its way west. First to the south, then the north, it undulates in a series of peaks and knobs. I've seen a few CDT markers, but they eventually lead off the crest to the north. It's too nice a day to leave the ridge; I'll stick to the high route for now. In this country, a trail only ties you down.

Too many folks ask me why I do these long walks. I enjoy the questions. It just strikes me as sad that they have to ask why. Are the winds of adventure and tastes of freedom so shackled that imagination can't grasp their existence? Of course, I usually answer the why question with my one-word answer: "Freedom."

Today that answer is confirmed, especially when I turn away from those wayward trail markers to follow my heart instead of my head. The backpack is my path to this freedom, but the real key is the will. I want to be here. I want to see what's over the next mountain. I want to be alone for days at a time, to bathe in icy mountain water, to go without the luxuries, to sleep on the ground and eat only what I can carry or forage along the way. I want to be able to change my direction if I feel like it, to sleep early or late and camp where I want, to take my time or not. *Wanting* to be here, with all the limitations and conditions that go with it, is what frees me. At least for the time I'm out here.

I laugh when I think of how we Americans live. We really know how to talk up our freedom, how great we have it. We expound in great length on our land of opportunities, our wealth and how easy we have it. And it's true. Our country is the land of honey. But how many of us take advantage of our great freedoms? We tie ourselves into routines and ways of thinking that feed on more, more, more. Overconsumption is a way of life. We shackle ourselves to the TV god, to the microwave mission, to the information super highway. As we deliver the rhetoric of freedom, we enslave our selves with useless things, patting each other on the back and assuring each other that we have it pretty good. But is it good if you can't leave it? Is it freedom when we can't take our time, when going slow is a crime? Is it freedom when our schedules and luxuries demand so much upkeep that we can't get away from them? And finally, is it freedom when we are afraid to go for a walk without a radio, a flashlight, or a gun?

I've got an old country song buzzing through my brain this morning. I can't get it out of my head.

Pleease release me, oh my darlin',
Release me and let me love again.

I'm crooning it through my nose, whining it out and stretching each mournful syllable. It carries me along, as free as a bird. Eventually the ridge becomes more rugged. Cliffed out, I drop into a couple canyons on the Idaho side, then back to Montana, following a series of elk trails to the northwest. It's easy walking through sometimes dense forest, and it feels good to be in the shade for a while. The day is getting hot. Several miles bring me to a dense stand of firs near the top of a series of sloped meadows. I make my camp in the island of trees, enjoying the room with a view.

Later, dinner occupies me for a time, but the meadows and their fine vista draw me back. Like a new rock, freshly down from the heights, I've rolled to rest. The last of the sun's searching beams filter through an ominous storm cloud that's floating my way. These rays of tilting light steal here and there amidst the dark masses, occasionally finding a hole to dart through, painting trails between Earth and Heaven. The clouds creep closer with a distant groan of thunder. Still as stone, I watch and wait.

I see the rain before I feel it. Sheets of dark blue fall earthward in wave upon wave. The air has become alive now. The charge it carries ties the clouds to the mountain to the rain. To me. More thunder, but not threatening. It seems far away and benign, a storm shaking its kinks out. The rain is racing now, jumping over the fields, the patches of forests, the mountains themselves. It seems to ride the charge, energized and anxious to get somewhere, anywhere, as long as it can move.

I can hear it before it arrives. A distant rustle, so faint I'm not sure what it is at first. But it's quick, and approaching fast. The rustle merges to a patter, to a loud splattering of clatter that leaps across the grass. The first drops hit me like bullets. They've fallen far and feel full and cold. My instinct is to run for the shelter of the trees, for the dryness of my tent. But my eyes are riveted on the field. As each drop of rain pounds down, the grasses bounce and nod. "Yes," they're saying, "we do enjoy this."

The drops, scouts for the torrents to come, are increasing. The rock moves. I stand and stretch, turning my face to the rain and attempting to catch a drop or two on the end of my tongue. When I step back into the forest, the sound of the rain diminishes. In my tent, though, I hear each drip and drop with clarity. I drift off to sleep amid this friendly patter of endless rain.

I've regained the divide and crossed Bannack Pass. After a clear morning the afternoon skies are now preparing for another thunderstorm. It builds faster than I anticipate, and soon the lightning is cracking with a vengeance. Divide Creek parallels the ridge below the Idaho side. Its canyon appears much safer at the moment. Heeding my instincts, I head for lower ground.

The slope is treeless, covered thick with sage. A series of deep gullies laces the hill. With the thunderstorm above giving incentive, I'm flying down the mountainside. Each step crushes the scent of sage into the moist air. The sweetness in turn adds a certain buoyancy to my step. I spring along, skipping over one gully, then another. I'm about to jump another tiny arroyo when two fawns leap out in front of me. In perfect unison they bound away, two graceful pogo sticks hopping into the distance.

The trail along Divide Creek leads me through a narrow, meandering canyon. I'm walking fast again, hoping to reach a likable place to camp before the rain starts in earnest. A few sprinkles are teasing me along. Just as the drops begin to pound down in sheets I come to a cliff with a good overhang. I hunker into the sheltered spot, munching a late lunch, listening to the rain singing into the Earth.

This steady rhythm of the rain is the only sound I hear. It has totally engulfed my little world. The rock over my head echoes the sound. Sometimes the sound is almost like the song of a stream. Voices murmur. Choirs chant. I tilt my head and listen closer, sure that I have visitors. But it's only the rain. It drones on and on.

My lunch break lingers and stretches. I study the maps and then the rain. A nearby cave draws my curiosity. Perhaps I can camp there for the night.

1981—SOUTHERN ARIZONA

The snow is starting to pile up at the mouth of the old mine tunnel. Two inches so far. The wind is howling out there, but in here it's but a distant moan. I lucked out in stumbling across this. My tent hasn't been dry for days and now, more snow. I was already in the midst of it, hardly able to see in the blinding whiteout, when I noticed the dark spot in the hillside next to me. Now it's been a few hours. I'm dry and warm. Though it's below freezing outside, this mine shaft taps the internal heat of the Earth. I'm positively cozy.

As the day slips away with the fading light, I light a candle and crawl into my sleeping bag. The book I've been rereading on this trip is Tolkien's The Hobbit. *I find where I've left off the night before and dig in. It's a wild adventure, and the hero finds himself deep in the caves of the orcs. Hmmmm. I glance over my shoulder and look into the darkness of the long tunnel disappearing into the bowels of the Earth. Naw!*

Back to the book, things get creepier. Dark shapes, strange sounds, evil things abound. I wonder where this tunnel goes? Shifting my position, I can see down the shaft. Judging from the warmth of the air, I bet it goes quite a ways back. No telling what kind of critters are crawling around down there.

I make another attempt to read. The literary adventure into the caves is dark and scary. My concentration strays. I keep looking down the tunnel into the dark. Something could be looking out at me and I'd never

know. Was that a noise? Orcs and goblins, they're only imaginary char-
acters. But isn't fiction always based on some facet of fact?

I close the book. This is one of my all-time favorites, but I think I'll
put it aside for tonight. Bilbo would understand.

I trot over to the cave's entrance and look in. The mouth is tiny. It'd be a tight squeeze. The floor is cluttered with rocks. Not much room for me, let alone my pack. It's not too appealing, so I run back to my lunch spot.

1981—CENTRAL ARIZONA

The rain is intense. Water is flowing off the bill of my cap like a miniature Niagara. It's hard to see anything. My feet plod onward, boots squishing with each step. Normally I'd stop in such a storm and put up the tent, but I recall an old mine shown on my topographical map. Perhaps there'll be another dry tunnel, like that spot a few weeks back.

Up ahead the rugged remains of an old cabin appear through the blinding deluge. Forty feet away, in the side of the canyon wall, is the framed entrance to the mine. Walking up to the dark opening, I have to crouch to look in. It looks muddy and has a strange smell. The space, as far back as I can see, looks cramped, damp, and uninviting.

A corner of the ruined cabin offers an appealing dry spot. No orcs or goblins here. I curl up and sleep well.

The morning dawns clear and crisp. I'm cooking breakfast over a fire in the little clearing in front of the tunnel. It's a peaceful morning. Just as I'm wondering what kind of sleep I'd have had in the tunnel, a large javelina wanders sleepily from the dark shaft. Spotting me, it bolts in panic, bellowing a series of warning grunts. Two more of the wild pigs race from the shelter of the mine, scrambling madly in all directions. I'm standing there, spoon in hand, bewildered by the entire scene. Strange bedfellows indeed.

The rain continues. I pull on my wool cap and down vest to fight the chill. I'll sit this out. I know it'll quit soon. No sense getting drenched when I have this dry nook to nestle in. I search the rock for signs of use. Has this spot ever been shelter to others? There are no signs of fire, blackened stone, or ashes. The rubble under the overhang looks as if it has fallen fairly recently. In fact, it looks like some of the ceiling is ready to cave in anytime now. Hmmm. Geological time ticks to a mighty slow clock. Surely another hour or two won't see any change. But it makes me wonder.

Rock Dream

Shaded from the sun,
I took welcome shelter under the ledge.
The dark slot in the smooth wall
Gaped like a giant's grin
And swallowed me whole.
When night came I stretched out under the rock,
The sandstone a few feet above my face,
And wondered when this shoulder would shrug,
Rocks crashing down,
Taking me back in one pulverizing smash.
I could feel it there,
Pressing down upon me,
Compressing my bones to fossil,
Dashing my brains to powdery dust
Blood oozing with the stone seams,
From that moment,
Forever destined to dream of rock,
My epitaph, sleeping
In the smooth canyon wall.

Minutes after the rain lets up I find the perfect campsite. Coming over a low knob, I nearly bump into a doe and a fawn. They're grazing on a little bench under several large Doug firs. The creek tumbles by in a narrow chute below. The two deer scatter at my approach, leaving me their tiny corner of paradise. How could I turn it down? Above me on both sides of the canyon are wonderful cliffs and rock outcroppings, even a natural arch. But most appealing is the flat spot, carpeted with fir needles, just big enough for my tent.

The morning brings clear skies with crisp, cold air for this narrow canyon. I decide to have a hot breakfast and let the day warm up a bit. The coals from my evening campfire (to save gas on this long stretch between resupply points) are still warm. In no time, I have another little fire going. The crackling blaze gives off minimal heat. Campfires generally aren't all that efficient. One side of the body fries while the other side freezes, but the cheer from that flickering flame is often more important than the warmth. The presence of the fire fuels our inner fires. It's something primal within all humans, something passed down intact in our genetic memory. The flames of the campfire often light a psychological warmth that is just as cozy as the heat emanating to our toes and outstretched fingers.

This morning I'm content to gaze into those tongues of fire, hugging my cup of tea, and letting my thoughts roam. A cozy warmth settles over my tiny camp. It'd be so easy to sit here all morning and just study those flames.

But the high country calls. The stream I follow is flowing strong, forming little falls and cascades on its way down the narrow canyon. The path is narrow and looks hardly traveled. Steps squeak on the wet grass. My breath joins in the rhythm, making little puffs of steam in the cold air. A squirrel chatters angrily at my noisy passing.

It's three miles up to Divide Lake. Those first miles slip by in no time. Soon, the canyon widens and the trail steepens. The land changes. I'm stepping into a subalpine environment. The lake is perfectly smooth, a mirror of steely green glass reflecting each contour, tree, and mountain surrounding the high basin. Here, each peak has two lives: one, the lofty summits, faces to the wind and snow, home to endless miles of sight; the other, hidden in the water's sheen, visible only in the lake's peace, blurred and hidden as the morning wears off into day.

I leave the pack to walk around the lake. A pika squeaks from the talus nearby. Trout swim slowly through the shallows along the water's edge, darting away at my passing shadow. From every shore the reflected mountains shine in perfection. The sight of the rocky summits is beautiful. Add the calm detail of the lake's mirror, and each peak and tree, no matter how humble, becomes a glorious statement of its own.

At one point, as I near the shore, I note my own reflection. It's something I don't see often out here. Crouching down for a closer look, I notice something different. I look older. Healthier, but older. A lot of wrinkles on that weathered face. I grin. It smiles back at me. I'd forgotten. Laugh, and it laughs, too. Stick out the tongue, and it wags its tongue back. I squish my face into the ugliest contortion I can compose. The reflection joins in. I wonder what a fish would think looking up at that. I toss in a pebble, following the ripples across the lake. They slowly fade into the smoothness of the surface. I glance back into my own reflection, the face not seeming nearly as old.

It's a short hike from the lake to the crest of the Continental Divide. Deadman Creek, just to the west (yet on the east side of the divide), will be my gateway to more rugged, wilder country. It will lead me directly into the core of the Italian Peaks.

Italian Peaks? Sounds a bit exotic, more than a touch foreign. It's a remote area, the southwesternmost loop of the Montana state line. It's a land of few visitors and holds more than its share of mystique. The Continental Divide trail markers detour around the area. I, myself, have cut this hidden corner from my route on two previous long treks. I've always told myself that I'd come back and take a closer look. What's in there? Today, I find out.

Upon reaching the crest, the trail leads me south onto an open bald. Here, I get my first close-up of what's in store. Deadman Creek is an arrow shooting straight to the heart of impressive cliffs, stunning walls of twisted rock, and rugged peaks. One mountainside is totally curled, the grain of the rock exposed to the canyon and portraying eons of thrusting, moving Earth. Magnificent is too mild a word to describe such mountains.

The grassy knoll is inviting, but the excitement is building. I've got to move. I want to get up into that high basin, to walk those meadows and climb those peaks. I descend to Deadman Creek and follow its canyon for a few miles. Gradually the creek dies out. The trees disappear. I enter a wide, rocky basin. The peaks of the divide loom above me like petrified waves, perched and ready to come crashing down. Every thirty yards I stop to gawk and shoot pictures. I keep muttering to myself, "This is great!"

The climb to the pass between Deadman and Nicholia Creeks is gradual. When I reach the broad saddle three mountain goats are making their precarious way across a sheer face above me. I watch them through my zoom lens for a half hour, until they're out of sight. Giant, fluffy whites float across the deep blue sky, casting shadows over the peaks. Nearby, Italian Peak changes with each minute, the racing shadows playing games with its portrait. The quality of stunning, in-your-face beauty surpasses that of many national parks. Who could experience it and not wish to preserve it? I can't understand why it has been left out of so many wilderness proposals. This is a national treasure.

In the upper basin of Nicholia Creek I leave the old pack trail and begin walking a series of game trails. The day is perfect. The hiking easy. I'm feeling charged. I could make a lot of miles, but I'd be leaving this wonderful basin. Instead, I turn back and make an early camp a couple hundred yards from a hidden spring. This entire corner of the basin seems hidden. It feels secluded and tucked away.

Once the camp is set up and my food securely tied in a tree, it's time to wander. I have no destination. I just want to see what's here, get a closer look. Inevitably, for me, this usually means climbing to a higher vantage point. I end up on one of the unnamed peaks, nested in the rocks, watching the place.

Much goes on before me. Clouds are dashing shadows in an array of changing mosaics over the surrounding mountains. A lone buck is grazing his way across a distant meadow. Three billy goats climb the crags nearby. This wild paradise has given me something. I feel connected here, like my roots have become securely bonded to the bedrock beneath me. With that tie comes a great strength. I notice that when I think of my mother's illness I'm thinking more positively. I'm thinking of how death fits in to the pattern around me, how I feel more able to cope with it, to bear up to whatever is going to come my way. The peace, the beauty, the wildlife, the entire mood of this quiet corner of Earth has me filled with a warm, glowing thankfulness. When I walk back down to my camp I feel as if my heart, along with every emotion in it, has just had the most soothing massage.

On the Mountain's Heights

*"You tramp across the ridgeline as the world
    spreads down below,
And you're feeling like a king, just a-hoarding over
    his gold.
You think that if you take another breath you'll
    just explode,
And you feel the choir a-singing in your soul."*
            from the song "All Along the Great Divide"

My pack feels good today, a bit lighter. I've used up four days of food since Monida Pass. It makes a lot of difference. Of course, in the morning the pack always feels light. Toward the day's end, after ten or fifteen miles, it tends not to feel so cozy.

I'm walking elk trails through a mature forest of subalpine fir and whitebark pine. These are good trails. There's a feeling of antiquity in walking here. Generation upon generation of the passing herds have used these routes. True, there are numerous blowdowns, and occasional steep ups and downs. Sometimes I must duck some fairly low limbs, but generally the tracks follow a contour along the path of least resistance. They spill me out on the crest of the divide three miles from my camp. Here I start over a series of minor peaks. It's slow going, not only due to the lack of a trail or roughness of terrain, but more to my own interest in the expansive views. I'm taking a lot of pictures but also just stopping to look about. Definitely a day for playing the tourist.

The day wears on. I take a long lunch break lying in the grass of a high saddle. The clouds are building, and the wind, too, as I set off again. I traverse a knob covered with a forest of twisted limber pines. These trees, both living and dead, are gnarly old things, weathered and molded by the wind. It's as if at one time they were all dancing and suddenly the music stopped, freezing them in one contorted position or another. Walking among them is like walking through an art gallery; trying to figure out just what it all means.

Breaking into the open again, I hear a distinct roar that causes me to search the skies. Somewhere, a jet is heading this way. Scanning the clouds, I look and look. No sign of it. Yet, the noise is close, and getting louder. I'm confused until a trace of motion in the canyon below me catches my eye. In disbelief I watch as the fighter shrieks through the narrow defile and within feet of the pass where I first crested the divide this morning. It screams through, a noisy slash across a priceless masterpiece.

I shout at the pilot, the words drowned in the sound of the low-flying war machine. I'm thinking of the goats, the elk, the tranquillity of the high basin where I spent last evening. Precious peace traded for the power hungry grin of a joyride. The silence will reclaim itself. It has a way of doing that. But it is a delicate thing, this wild place. The airspace above is just as important as the earth below. Like a sailboat the wildlands need both the water and the air. Punch enough holes in any boat and it will sink. Scratch the wilderness too thin and it ceases to be wilderness.

As the clouds begin to rumble, I step back into Montana and descend into the basin of Bear Creek. A herd of a hundred elk stampedes over the ridge to the south, dirt flying and dust billowing. A few of the bulls pause to stare, then bolt after the main herd. In moments, the entire herd has vanished.

The jet would have startled these elk, too, but I wonder about my own impact in setting them off. Can a human come into a place like this and not affect what's here in some way? Someday, when we as a species have gained a little humility, we should set aside areas that are totally off limits for any of us: "No Humans Allowed." Areas that will be true preserves of unaltered biological function. This would not only give the place back to itself, but it would give humankind a special dream, a place for our imaginations to play with. What could be more romantic, more inspiring, than a blank spot way out there?

Tonight I'm content to fill in the blanks that were the Italian Peaks. I put up the tent in a small stand of subalpine fir, looking out on the open hills of the basin. A few drops of rain, a quick bath, dinner, a short walk, and I still can't stand to see this day slip away.

~

I've been singing in my sleep. Song dreams. They come to me a lot out here. In the dream they're always the best of songs: memorable tunes and inspiring lyrics. Unfortunately, I can never remember any details in the morning, but I always awake feeling good after a night of dream singing. This morning I must have been singing pretty loud. I woke myself up.

There's not much light yet, just the faint half-light floating between night and day. Enough to see, but no detail. A faint rosiness colors the eastern horizon. As I watch, a thin strip of gray turns to silver, hinting of some colossal movement beyond those far mountains. I should get to a better vantage point.

After grabbing a vest, the tripod, and the camera, I head up the ridge. Ten minutes gets me up to a good bench. I turn to the east and wait. And wait. For a moment I'm anxious. What if it doesn't come? But no, I can see a change in the pink hues. The silver line on the crest of the far mountain is shinier. The day is coming.

A thousand sunrises, a thousand different paintings, a thousand inspired mornings, a thousand prayers of thankfulness. I watch and wait. Colors build and change. Shadows bend and blend. The horizon brightens. The layer of silver turns to yellow, then orange. A brilliant orb, a torch of a sun, creeps slowly over the mountain.

I've picked my spot well. The first rays fall squarely on my face. I close my eyes and tilt my head higher into the warm beams. How rich I am! How precious, these first beams of a new day. Stretching like a cat, I rise up and spread my arms toward the new sun, a reverent embrace. A song spills out.

> *Live each day like you mean it,*
> *Grab hold of each dawn that comes your way.*
> *And if it's blessings you're a-countin'*
> *Try a mornin' in the mountains,*
> *There ain't no better way to start the day.*

Later, as I return to my camp, I'm thinking of my mother, far to the east, and how good those morning rays could have felt to her.

Today I will climb Eighteen-Mile Peak. I'm excited about it. It's the third highest mountain in this corner of the state, 11,141 feet. I've been climbing lots of mountains these past weeks, unnamed and unknown for the most part. This one has inspired someone enough to tag it with a name. The title is pretty nondescript, but at least it's something. Somehow that gives it a bit more appeal, a little more pizzazz.

Back on the divide, I'm glad to find the skies clear to the west of me. The route is high and exposed for the next several miles. I wouldn't want to be walking this on a stormy day.

Last summer Leslie and I walked hundreds of miles above tree line in Colorado. We'd plan it so we'd be off the crest by one or two o'clock when the afternoon storms rolled in. The storms didn't bother us much at first, but throughout the summer, as we walked north, we heard more lightning stories. As soon as folks heard we were walking the divide, the conversation would take a morbid twist and another tale of fried hikers would come spilling out. I came to dread encounters with other hikers because of this. I'd watch Leslie's face as she soaked it all in. Her eyes would get a bit wider, but she wouldn't say much. Not until we were off again by ourselves. Then, inevitably, she'd start worrying aloud about our next stretch above tree line. Sometimes even on a nearly cloudless day, when a distant cloud would appear, she'd make a comment about lightning. It got to be a joke, but a serious one.

One day as we walked a seven-mile stretch above the trees the clouds caught up with us. Thunder began shaking the mountains. We were walking fast. I was ahead. A bit off the trail the carcass of a horse lay bloated and stinking. I walked over for a closer look. A hole was burned in its flank, an enormous, lightning-burnt hole. When Leslie came up the trail I waved her on. "Just some dead horse." I never told her it was a lightning victim. I would never have been able to keep up with her.

Today is perfect. No lightning today. No Leslie, either. I wish she were here. This is her kind of place. It feels wild. The ridge narrows to a rocky spine, a knife edge cutting through the bluest sky. At each side the world falls off to wide, flat valleys. This rough backbone, like that of a sleeping dragon, takes me higher and higher. Two thousand feet of elevation from my camp up to the summit. It slips steadily away.

Climbing a mountain is many things. Some days it is a pilgrimage, an act of faith. Other days it becomes a workout, an exercise of muscle and bone, a contest of body and soul. Today, the act is one of luxury.

I am indulging myself. I don't need to climb this peak. It'd be just as easy to go around it. That's what the pioneers did. They had no use for these rocky crags. The high mountains were just barriers, just masses of earth forcing a wide detour. A person who climbs a mountain must have the luxury to take the time. Mountains can't be rushed. They must be savored. They are often the shortest distance between two points, yet the longest route in terms of time. To invoke a bit of Robert Frost, they are "the road less traveled." They are the other path, the longer, more difficult one. The one that is not necessary for the majority, but holds a reverent fascination for the rest.

I wonder about Eighteen-Mile Peak. I can see more than eighteen miles from its summit. In fact, the view encompasses hundreds of square miles, but it must be eighteen miles from somewhere. A study of the maps only widens the question. There is an Eighteen-Mile Creek. Perhaps the creek is eighteen miles from somewhere and the peak was named after the creek. Or perhaps Frederich von Eichtenmille discovered the peak back in 1848 on his way to inventing highway mile markers. Yes, that clears it all up.

Some mountaintops are broad and fat. You could have a basket-ball game atop them. But here on Eighteen Mile we have a peak that is worthy of the name. The mountain has a focus. All corners come together in a fine point of jutting rock with a small flat spot on which to sit and enjoy the converging forces of earth and sky. Here, suspended in the heights, I feel like an eagle on a lofty perch, gazing out over half of Idaho.

The view is one of those sights you don't want to take pictures of, knowing you can never hope to capture on film what the vista is playing in your heart. A skip away to the west of me is Jump Mountain. It also is a sharp-topped peak, lower than here, but with a chillingly steep face. Beyond it lies the gaping Lemhi Valley and then all the ranges of central Idaho. The valley is dull, dusty brown with thin ribbons of green, like veins in a leaf, showing every trace of surface water. One of my favorite trail towns, Leadore, lies sprawled across the north end. Such a big splash for such a tiny town. Southward the brown of the valley disappears into the blue haze of the Snake River Plain. Like ghosts, two cinder cones are barely visible, hanging in the air over the harsh desert.

Behind me, eastward, are the familiar landmarks of ranges I've walked. Here on the peak, goat hair lies scattered like patches of new-fallen snow clumped among the rocks. I can picture the goats lounging here, looking out on the miles, lazing in the heat of the sun. It is what I do today, sprawled against my leaning pack. But unlike the goats, I add a touch of music. The guitar sounds good here. So does my voice. Real mountain music.

I come here searching for my share of dreams,
Looking for songs on the way,
And the tunes that I heard, were all sung without words
But the wild wind sure had its say.
I heard the coyotes question, and the elks answered call,
The bluebirds sing to the water's sweet fall,
And the Earth sang her blessing to each one and all,
With her windsong.

Later, I notice a plastic bottle hidden in the summit cairn. It's a register. The entries are spread over several years and don't show a whole lot of folks traveling this way. Yet, some of these names I know. Friend and author George Wuerthner shows up on one page. On another, Cedron Jones, a staunch wilderness supporter from Helena. Also a fellow by the name of Kim Boone, a long-distance hiker whom I met several years ago in the Madison Range. His entry mentions sleeping on the peak. Another visitor counted thirteen goats sharing the summit when they arrived.

The hours creep by, and I begin to get restless. There is a phenomenon with mountains. Getting up to the top is always easier than getting down. I've been eyeing the north ridge. That's the way I want to go, continuing along the Continental Divide. The first hundred yards or so look absolutely menacing—a sawtooth of giant rock slabs and blocks tilted every which way. The teeth are ragged and crumbly. To either side the mountain drops off a thousand feet. It looks dangerous. Scary. I've been trying to ignore it. I've been playing my guitar, stretching out a snack break, studying the maps. Basically stalling. Finally, with a sigh, I jump to my feet and hoist the pack. Time to get to it.

I step deliberately off the summit. It seemed so solid, so connected to the Earth. I've traded that security for boulders and blocks the size of refrigerators and Volkswagens, appliances ready to drop off into oblivion at any moment.

Inching. Baby stepping. Reaching. Jumping. Grabbing. Hanging. Praying. I'm slowly making my way into the dragon's teeth. The big gaps force me to hang and drop, or dangle blindly trying to find a foothold, all with the bulky pack on my back. Several times I stop, too scared to keep going. A few deep breaths and I try it again.

This is crazy. I'm in a notch I can't get over or around. It isn't going to work. Looking back the way I've come is just as intimidating. Can't go forward, and I sure don't want to go back. Great! What now?

I decide to go off the west side, down a precipitous boulder field, across the side of the slope below the "teeth" on the ridge, and then climb back to the crest beyond the sawtooth. Sounds easy enough.

I descend carefully into the rubble of loose boulders. Rocks the size of suitcases lie spilled across the slope, balanced precariously atop each other, poised and ready to crash down the slope. The angle is steep. My arm bangs on the rocks. It's easy to touch the side of the mountain without stretching too far. Talking to myself, I try to force a chuckle. "OK, Jim. You're getting close to nature now!" It doesn't seem very funny.

I'm doing a lot of talking right now, talking myself through this whole thing. Trying to lighten my fear. "Let's step here. Good. Now over here." But throughout the conversation the exclamation of "Oh, shit!" keeps popping up.

The entire rock slope seems ready to take off and go at the least provocation. If it does, it won't stop until it reaches the canyon floor 2,000 feet down. I'm trying not to think about those tons of stone. Trying not to think about those 2,000 feet. Instead, I focus on each step. The rocks groan and slip fractions of an inch, complaining of being kept up here when gravity calls from the canyon floor. These creaks and moans are nerve wracking, as if my own chatter is being answered in kind.

I'm trying not to breathe too hard, as if even that may set the slope off. Sometimes I hold my air in for a step or two, letting it out in a big gasp when I have a firm footing for a moment. Several times I step onto boulders that begin to roll. In that split second I wince, pray, and jump to the next rock all in one motion. These rollers only shift six or eight inches and then stop, wedged in tighter against the masses. They make me want to stop and listen for a minute. Sometimes I can hear the rock voices from underneath, inner groanings, for a moment or two after these sudden shiftings.

Time has a way of expanding in a situation like this. A second seems like a minute, one minute turns to five. I have no idea how long it takes me. It seems like half a day. I suppose it's more like forty-five minutes. Once I'm standing on solid mountain again I turn back to look at what I can see of the slope. I dub it "The Field of Death" and laugh. It's easier to laugh now.

The ridge offers smooth sailing beyond the toothlike section. I reach the flat summit of Cottonwood Mountain with no difficulty at all. Here, the crest broadens into a wide grassy ridge sloping gradually downward to the northwest. The footing is good and the wide panoramas have me euphoric. The smooth, parklike ridge is dotted here and there with outcroppings of rock, blocks of stone jutting from the mountain, kind of a Rocky Mountain Stonehenge. As I tramp down the gently tilting divide, I approach one of these stone piles. Behind the rocks, on the downhill side, I note two bucks, their presence betrayed by their tall racks protruding several inches over the block of rock. For a moment I think of stopping and taking out the camera, but I've been shooting all day. This sight will be for me, rather than the camera. I don't even pause in my stride.

This moment of rounding the huge rock and turning to look upon the deer is one of those frozen in time flashes that will always be ingrained in my most precious of memories. As I step around the corner the two bucks turn their heads toward me, one of them looking over his shoulder. The sun behind them is peeking through a sky of fluffy white clouds. Its rays slant down and through the velvet of the antlers, setting each rack aglow with a golden light, perched like haloes upon bodies so taut each muscle seems ready to burst from the skin.

For one precious second I am allowed this sight. The deer are frozen in this pose, highlighted in an aura of gold, tense and ready to spring. Of course, they do bolt. But for me they will always be in that frame of light, that split second of time when I turned the corner of the huge rock.

Sometimes I think of the conscious decision not to take the picture. At the time, I didn't realize exactly what picture I'd be passing up. I didn't deliberate fully on the concept of leaving the sight to my heart rather than my eye. I often recall the sight of those two deer. I know now that the image I hold in my memories is much more intense than any I could possibly have captured on film.

The Continental Divide trail markers show up a mile later on the saddle above Meadow Creek. I'm surprised to see them again. The official trail has cut off the entire Italian Peaks region. I'm glad that fewer people will be funneled into the area, but I know that most places are only preserved when folks know about them. Like politicians, wild areas need a base of support, a constituency. I'm glad of these days alone in this place, yet like many of these areas I've been walking, I wonder how long it can stay wild if folks don't know about it.

A mile later I take the wrong ridge. The mistake is obvious when I get high enough to see both ridges, but like many wrong turns it ends up being the right way. At least for the moment. I spot a herd of forty elk. Just above the herd, close to where I stand, a golden eagle launches itself from the mountainside, flapping wings, a graceful wave of slow motion.

Another few miles, another herd of a hundred elk, and I descend Coyote Creek to a campsite in the forest. A light sprinkle of rain sets the canyon alive with smells. Later I cook dinner over a fire and sing to the darting tongues of flame, occasionally throwing on a sprig of sage. Bats dive every which way, snapping up mosquitoes. Sometimes I can hear them flit by my ears. They're good navigators. They never hit me. I'm glad.

Wild Rockies Home

"There ain't no rhyme to this reason,
The key to all is the changing season,
It takes us in and gives us back,
Written there in them fading tracks."
*   —from the song "Thinkin' Like A Mountain"*

It's been five days since I've seen any people. Five days of solitude. That word "solitude" is a warm, soothing word for me. It is a sharing, a blessing, a time for spiritual contemplation and prayer. It is a place where I have been dwelling. I count these days alone, hoarding them like a squirrel storing nuts for wintry days ahead. But today is a Saturday. I will have to share some of my stash. I don't mind my encounters with people; in fact, I look forward to them. But these solo times are surely something special to be valued.

Morrison Lake has never struck me as an especially pretty lake. I've camped twice on its shores, but only because that's where I ended up on those days of walking. Tucked up against the Montana side of the divide, it's the place where I expect to see people. And I do, but today I see something else.

The lake looks different to me today. As I approach from the south I'm struck by the green shades of the water. No, not green. I guess it's more of a blue. No, that's not right either. Actually, some parts are deep blue, others an emerald green. Other areas mix the two into various shades of rich turquoise and colors with fancy names. Along one stretch of the eastern shore the water has a red tint. When I get closer I see it's from the water plants growing there.

This isn't how I remembered this place. The peaks of the divide, the bare rock glaring in the sun, reflect in the surface of the multicolored waters. Today the lake is hauntingly beautiful. Someone has made a camp on the south shore. No one's around as I walk by. On the northeast corner, I start to pass above a truck parked down near the shore. A man is fishing while his wife lies sunning on a lawn chair. She's wearing a bikini. I couldn't help but notice.

They're nice people. Terry and Sheryl from Missoula. Terry is interested in my treks. I ask him if he'd mail some letters to Leslie and Mom for me. While I address the stamped envelopes I've carried with me, he offers me a soda and more fuel for my stove. I tell him about my trip and ask him what's going on in the world. He says something about a new war, Iraq attacking Kuwait, or something like that. We trade stories for over an hour. It's a nice meeting.

~

I'm walking a jeep trail now. It leads me back to the top of the Continental Divide, the Bitterroot Range, the Beaverhead Mountains, and along the crest for several miles. The ridge here is broad and mostly open. I can see for miles, but not as far as yesterday. It's hot, and the heat adds a shimmering haze to the sky. It makes me tired, too.

The spring where I want to get water is surrounded with cows. This herd is used to seeing people—they don't run off when I walk up. I have to push my way through to the water. The place is a mess. The grass is gone, the bare earth worn away. It looks like a bulldozer has been at work. The water itself trickles out of a rusty pipe. I fill up my waterbag, nearly three gallons, while the cows gather round me in a semicircle, staring with baleful eyes. With my belt I tie the bag atop my pack. It rides like a dog in a pickup, shifting from one side to the other. Heavy, too.

I go only another mile. There's a nice spot right on the crest of the divide. No need for the tent tonight. There's a thunderstorm down in the Italian Peaks, but up here it's clear. The pack is propped up with my walking stick. I use it as a backrest while I eat dinner, and later as I play music.

The evening slips away and soon the sun is a fiery orange ball bouncing off the crest of the Lemhi Range. I walk up to a higher viewpoint and hunker down. The air is still, the world silent. My breathing seems to be the only sound for miles. My body seems so small in this grand expanse, yet with this setting sun my soul feels as big as the universe I am a part of. The phrase "peace on Earth" runs endlessly through my head.

Just as I'm counting my blessings, wondering what could be better, a glance over my shoulder makes me jump. The moon, nearly full, is rising in the east. It looks huge and exceptionally close. In fact my first thought is that it's crashing into the Earth. As I watch, it slowly rises higher over the mountains. This is a nice phenomenon, the sun going down on one side of me, the moon coming up on the other. It's hard to decide which way to turn. Like a battle for glory, each heavenly body puts on its classiest face. The lighting is spectacular.

Of course, the moon eventually wins out. At least, for now. The sun sets. The moon rises. The fine, delicate moonlight, warm and sincere, lights the peaks and hills. Moon magic.

I walk back down to my bivouac. With reverence I lift the guitar, place the strap around my shoulder, and walk back to the knob. The views of the day are now the views of the night, every mountain, valley, and ridge painted in the white light of moonbeams. When I play, the song is one of the moment. I've never heard it before. Each note rings and then sets out into the night, slipping away and into the stillness. I try to follow the notes as they float away on the moon's rays, but like bats they flit here and there and are swallowed in silence.

Circling the knoll, I play a wordless song to each direction, again and again. The moon has me now. I wander the ridge, still playing, to another knob. And then another. I feel as if I could play myself to the top of each mountain in the range tonight, but I settle for three, strung out over a mile along the crest. Words start floating with each note out across the moonbeams. I add one line and then another, singing them over and over. They change and change again with each singing. A couple hours later when I return to my camp, I have a new song. The moon is bright enough that I am able to write it down by the moonlight.

Up in Montana the moon's shining bright,
Out over the Bitterroot Mountains tonight,
There's an owl out there hootin', and she's calling to you.
It's straight to your heart, and you know that it's true.

Come walk with me out in the hills
We'll sing in the mountain rain
We'll drink of them clear, sweet rollin' waters
Learn the song of the open plain,
Come walk with me out in the sun
Out where the wild ones still roam
And we'll be walkin' free, you and me,
Out in my Wild Rockies Home.

I've been a-ramblin' this land far and wide,
The wind is my trail, the raven's my guide,
The mountain before me welcomes me in,
But only the coyote knows where I've been.

I know that it's foreign, this life that I live.
But there's something in a mountain that a dollar can't give,
It's a taste of the wild that's my right at birth,
It's a place in the circle, the song of the Earth.

Come walk with me out in the hills,
Sing in the mountain rain,
We'll drink of them clear, sweet rollin' waters
Learn the song of the open plain,
Come walk with me out in the sun,

160

Out where the wild ones still roam.
And we'll be walkin' free, you and me,
Out in my Wild Rockies Home,
Out in my Wild Rockies Home.

The ground shakes. One thump, then another sneak through the cloak of my consciousness. A flurry of rhythm as I come totally awake whispers the presence of a deer bounding away, having come upon my sleeping form. I roll over. The eastern horizon is still dark but for a thin tinge of lightening gray. A few stars are still visible in the sky. Sunrise is still a long way off.

I lie there, wide awake. It seems like I just dozed off. I was up late last night with that bright moon, singing for a time, then just lying in the bag for hours looking at the stars. If I'd been able to stay awake all night, I would have. The entire universe was in my grasp, all there, just spread out as if a big box of sparklies had been knocked over and spilled into every nook and cranny of the heavens. It humbled me. It stretched me. It touched me somewhere beyond myself. It was the best church service I could ever attend.

Today is Sunday, I just realized. There will be a lot of families heading to church this morning. Lots of complaining kids. How I hated to put on Sunday clothes when I was a boy. Mom was always very particular about how we looked when we went to church. It seems like we spent more time getting dressed for church than we spent actually in church. My favorite part of Sunday was visiting with family and friends once we got home from the service.

It's strange—all those years of going to church as a youngster and all those years of saying the blessing for our evening meals, and I can't once remember talking to Mom or Dad about God. No heart-to-heart, this-is-what-I-believe conversations. Perhaps church was supposed to fill that void. I never thought much about it, but my spiritual growth has grown in direct proportion to my time in the wild country and away from religion. Religion, humans' attempts at explaining, regulating, and even claiming God, is often confusing for me. Even after a time of studying several faiths. Some things make more sense when we accept the fact that we cannot explain everything, not even in spiritual terms. Thus spirituality is a personal thing for me. It wears no title and can't be confined in boxes, books, or even churches. It's a faith I've soaked up from the months in the mountains, the years in the desert, and the nights under the starry sky. Today I'll be going to church like millions of others around the world, but it's the Church of the Universe, the one I attend every day.

My days are often begun like this, mulling over myriad thoughts from the comfort of my bag. The sun is taking its time. The morning has a chilly bite to it. Only a bit of my face peeks from the confines of my down comfort. A mosquito hums an approach.

Mosquitoes, taken one at a time, are actually fascinating creatures. I find this out when this one comes in for a landing on my left nostril. If I close my right eye I can get a good look at this guy. Or is it a gal mosquito? It's hard to tell, they're so small. Actually, my friend Lloyd Sumner tells me that only female mosquitoes bite, needing a blood meal for their eggs.

I'm not surprised that the mosquito landed on my nose. It stands out like the Empire State Building from my face. To a mosquito it probably reads like a giant billboard, "Land Here!" It's interesting, this closeup look at the skeeter. Although the intimate detail of the legs, body, and head are all there to study, I can't help but focus on its most infamous appendage, the proboscis. That long sword pokes and prods my beefy nose, testing the texture, and like a dowser, searching for just the right place to drill.

I twitch my nose and give a blow out of the corner of my mouth when the mosquito starts to get serious. She flies up and over to the right nostril, a distant journey up and over the Matterhorn. I close my left eye. The entire routine is repeated.

This goes on for some time, me foiling the mosquito's attempts to draw any of my blood. It gets to know the terrain of my nose quite well. Also my forehead and cheeks. Twice, the little bug flies over my mouth and is launched into space with a spout of hot air. Eventually she flies away, on to easier pickings.

The morning reverie resumes, but when the sun slips suddenly over the horizon in a blaze of new warmth, I begin to move. A quick breakfast, a few minutes to pack up my bag, and I'm off again, up the divide.

Mountains are alive in the mornings, more so than at any other time of day. Not only with the questing golden light of dawn, but with the creatures who dwell here. On the calm morning air, sound carries and rings with a sharp newness. Each bird song dances on bright scents of sage and pine. In the valley, coyotes yip and bark on the hunt. The excitement in their voices vibrates with anticipation. Nearby, a herd of elk pounds away at my approach, the rumble of their passing echoes over the ridge.

When I reach the summit of Horse Prairie Mountain, it is already occupied. A large buck mule deer is unsure of what to make of me. He starts to turn down the slope but then stops and returns. My presence is puzzling for this guy. For twenty minutes he debates the merits of retreating or not. He skirts the knob I sit on, running to one side, staring me down, then wandering purposefully to a better vantage point.

Today is a lazy day. I feel no pressing destination, no need to hike long and hard. On the rocky summit of Horse Prairie Mountain I pull out the guitar. The buck is really confused now. It's too much for him, and he disappears into the forest as I add my own sounds to the morning music along the Great Divide.

The frost is sparklin' on the meadow,
Sunlight filters through the pines
The mountains are alive and so are we
Walkin' hand in hand with mornin' time.

The ridge becomes a series of grassy knobs crested with remnant crowns of jagged rock. Across the dull green slopes, a fluff of creamy white is walking my way. The mountain goat stops and rubs his head in a clump of sage. While his head is down, I move closer, then freeze. He wanders along the ridge, stopping to rub again. I move closer still.

When he raises his face this time, he looks right into mine, staring hard for nearly a minute, then begins to walk away. That's the way I'm going, so I follow. For a mile and a half I follow. Over the ridge, around the knobs, a short cut here, a viewpoint there; I follow this lone goat. He stops and looks back occasionally. Sometimes waits. The ridge splits and I follow him along the divide. I don't even have to look at the map. I know I'm going the right way. I've lived this before. I'm not surprised.

The day is getting hot. The steep downhill is wearing on me. I finally stop for lunch in the shade of what looks like the last tree for seven miles. It's cool here. A slight breeze runs its fingers through my hair. The divide is clearly visible for miles. The ridge has become a desert. Heat waves ripple. It looks dull and barren, a faded brown from this height. Prickly pear country.

The heat has zapped me. I'm feeling lethargic, and I'm not excited about the next several miles. The lunch "break" turns to a lunch "stop," and then to a lunch "nap." When I awake and scan the open ridge below me, a smudge of life moves ever so slightly, tiny dots that perk my interest. Nothing wild would be moving about in the hot sun this time of day. Hmmm. The only creature stupid enough to be out here would be . . . humans?

My first thought is other hikers. Maybe some CDT hikers! The thought of meeting other long-distance hikers gets me up and walking in a flash. The specks are heading toward Deadman Pass. I want to reach it before they do in case they leave the divide there. I'm hiking fast. The heat isn't bothering me now that I'm moving. I haven't seen any other hikers during this entire trek except for planned encounters. The anticipation of visiting with other walkers has me in a merry mood.

The distant specks, which I still haven't positively identified as human, are now out of sight. I keep walking, scanning the ridge and the valleys to the east and west. Nothing. The closer I get to the pass, the more disappointed I get. Overlooking the empty pass, I wonder seriously if I was just seeing things. Or maybe it was just some deer. But then I see them.

Three hikers are moving slowly along the creek bottom, paralleling the divide on the Idaho side. I'm already a bit north of them, and far, far above them. I resign myself to missing them and watch as they walk slowly southward. One looks like he's having trouble. The figure keeps bending over as if he's being sick. The other two figures stand awkwardly around trying not to look at their puking partner. One of them finally notices me. I wave. They wave back. My only people experience of the day.

The miles from Deadman Pass over to Bannock Pass are easy, flat, ridge-walking miles, but they are hard miles for me today. With the incentive to meet other hikers gone, I'm feeling tired and hot again. My mind wanders. My feet plod automatically onward. At Bannock Pass I come to a gravel road. I walk into the middle and stop. This pass received much use in the days before the automobile. Used by various Indian tribes in their wide-flung travels, this pass also once had a railroad that carried cargo and passengers from Salmon to Dillon. Today, the main roads take advantage of other passes. Bannock Pass is quiet. I walk north without seeing any traffic.

By now I'm exhausted. The last few miles have dragged me down. I'm back in the trees. It's somewhat cooler, but I need to find water before I stop for the night. Wagonbox Spring is shown on my map. It's been my goal all day. I'm hot and dirty, dry and tired. The thought of the spring is all that keeps me going. I picture a deep trough with a pipe gushing out a stream of clear, icy water, the kind of place a guy could stick his head into and drink it dry. The image powers my faltering steps.

Up ahead I see the spring. It's fenced off, so I leave the pack, climb the fence, and trot over to the gray weathered boards of the spring box. It's bone dry. I'm in shock. I'm mad. I want to cry, curse, scream. I manage the cursing part without difficulty. Back at my pack, I throw myself onto the ground, rip off my heavy boots, and drink the last few swallows of water in my bottle. I'm afraid to look at the map. When I do, it looks like a long four miles to the next possible water. On top of the seventeen I've already done today, those four miles look like forty. But there is only one thing to do. Go on.

For twenty minutes I lounge in the shade near the dry spring, picking seeds from my socks, airing my hot feet, and generally pumping myself up for the next long pull. When I get going again, I'm ready for those four miles. The jeep trail I'm walking leads me around a bend. Standing there in the sun a quarter mile from the dry spring box is a deep trough with a gushing pipe of cold water. So much for knowing where I am. I walk to its side and dunk my head in the clear, frigid liquid. Wagonbox Spring at last.

~

I'm walking through a forest, ducking limbs, squeezing through the tightly spaced trees, glancing now and then at the compass held firmly in the palm of my hand. This is Grizzly Hill. There are no views. The broad, forested mountain forces me to trust the little magnet in my hand. Winding my way among the trees I spot three deer. A great horned owl swoops silently away when I walk too close to its perch. This feels good in here. Only one thing is missing.

There are no grizzlies on Grizzly Hill. I can imagine some shepherd coming upon one here years ago and probably killing it. Surely there must be some bear story behind the name. The grizz have been gone from this part of the divide for some time. I miss them. The more I think about it, the stronger my longing. Their absence creates a blank spot calling to be filled. Why have a place called Grizzly Hill if there are no grizzlies left to roam there?

Humans like to name things after animals, especially critters as bold and as beautiful as the grizzly bear. Here in Montana we have many businesses, teams, roads, and even subdivisions named after this most wonderful of North American mammals. California has a grizzly bear on their state flag. I'm thinking of all the folks who use that name, who wave that flag. How nice it would be for the bear to have their support, to have that many folks interested in bringing the bear back to places where he rightfully belongs. Places like Grizzly Hill.

A couple miles later the divide narrows, and for a time I'm walking the trace of a jeep trail. The day is warming up; I'm slowing down. I cross two knobs covered with ghost trees. Blown down by some fierce, fistlike wind long ago, they lie facing the same direction, root systems propped up on display, poised like huge anchors. The years of sun and wind have bleached the wood skeletons to a fine white and pink, the grain polished to an almost glossy finish. The roots, though upright, still seem rooted, frozen to the mountain and growing with each passing year, growing toward something more solid than mere wood, closer to the stone that holds the mountain up.

As I approach Goat Mountain, a new trail leads me on to the forested Montana side to a tiny creek. It's cool and shady here; the mossy rocks drip a lush green. The water is icy. I dunk my head in and it hurts. In the distance, I hear a curious beeping sound. As it gets closer I realize that what I'm listening to is an elk calf, a strange bleating mew that cries again and again. The sound gets louder, and suddenly the calf is coming down the trail toward me. Crying the entire time. Without seeing me, the calf walks to within thirty feet before turning, still bleating, still looking for Mom.

Back on the crest, I find myself walking a jeep trail through wide meadows, then forests of whitebark pine. The views are stunning, but the heat is wearing me down. I should have stocked up on water at the creek. Up here it's dry. I keep walking, looking for a spring.

Eighteen miles. Twenty miles. This is turning into a long day. By the time I descend to approach Lemhi Pass, the sun is sinking low. I've come nearly twenty-five miles. I'm beat. So tired that I feel punchy. I dream and think, not sure where thought ends and dream begins.

I'm almost to the pass. The ridge here is coated with tall, golden grass. A spikehorn muley springs up in the yellow light, but then pauses, freezing like a statue in the mellow tone of the setting sun as I walk steadily by. The buck is a part of the evening, catching up the precious golden light, gleaming clean, his antlers bent together like a pair of tongs, glowing in the richness of the ending day. Nearby, a doe freezes in the sage, poised solemnly in the surreal light. I walk by pretending not to see her.

The sun is dropping fast. I'm hitting my stride, feeling stronger now with my second wind. I have the camera out, shooting the sunset as it sinks through a layer of clouds, comes free, and is at last gobbled by the distant mountains.

A one-lane dirt road crosses the divide at Lemhi Pass. It doesn't get much traffic. I'm surprised to see a van parked at the pass. As I walk by, my greeting is returned with genuine warmth. Soon I'm chatting away with Mark and Nancy Jo Jander from Massachusetts. They're spending their summer retracing the path of the Lewis and Clark expedition, which crossed the divide here in August one hundred and eighty-five years ago. I haven't seen anyone all day. Yesterday, I saw just the distant hikers near Deadman Pass. It feels good to gab, especially with such nice folks. Nancy Jo is setting a table and invites me to join them for dinner. It's a magical evening. We're sitting on the crest of the continent, dining under the big, wide western sky, discussing Lewis and Clark. As we're finishing, the full moon comes rising. I pull out my guitar and sing.

So if your life has gone stale, how about hittin' the trail,
And leaving your streetlights behind,
Because that high country wind, is a-singin' again
Through the Montana moon in the pines.
Montana moon in the pines.

Just a couple hundred yards down the Montana side is a little roadside park. It has a few picnic tables, a spring, and an outhouse.

That's where I'll spend the night. After I thank the Janders and bid them farewell, I head off down the road. The moon still hasn't lit this part of the mountain. It's very dark. I don't have a flashlight. I feel my way along the road toward the little park, using my walking stick as a blind man uses a cane. It seems to get darker as I get closer into the crook of the mountain. I know I'm close. There's got to be a picnic table around here somewhere. I wonder if anyone else is camped here. Don't want to trip over anybody. With my feet, I probe and step, feeling my way down a hillside, around a few trees, and onto a little gravel pad. The table at last, and not occupied. I lay my bag out on the table top and crawl in. It's been a long day.

I awake feeling like I've slept for a year. I must have been more tired than I thought. The little picnic area is a delight. The sun is tilting through the big lodgepole pines. Birds of all kinds are singing up a storm. As I'd hoped last night, I do have it to myself, both of the tables and choice of two outhouses. A big sign tells me that this park was built by the Daughters of the American Revolution in honor of Sacajewea. I'm thinking a lot about her this morning. Lewis and Clark, too. I've read many books about these explorers, pored over their journals. The Janders's trip and being in this place where the expedition first crossed the Continental Divide have rekindled my sharp interest. When I wander over to a tiny spring trickling from the mountain, I'm pleased to find another sign with an entry from Captain Lewis's journal. The advance party under Lewis had reached here on August 12, 1805. He wrote:

> Two miles below McNeal had exultantly stood with a foot on each side of this little rivulet and thanked his God that he had lived to bestride the mighty and heretofore deemed endless Missouri.

I'm still thinking about Lewis and Clark, Sacajewea, and McNeal when I break camp and head back up to the pass. Many people don't know that Meriwether Lewis ended up taking his own life several years after returning to the East. Some folks think it was because of a broken heart over a lost love, but this morning I'm wondering if perhaps it wasn't just a let-down for him to spend three years of his life exploring and living in the wilderness, naming rivers and walking free under the western sun, then returning to a civilization he no longer felt a part of. How could life after that incredible journey be as exciting or as challenging? I don't think he could take the tame life that awaited his return.

The Janders are long gone, as I knew they would be. The road down the west side of the pass looks very narrow and extremely steep. I'm glad I'm sticking to the divide. My first few miles are on a one-lane logging road. There is no traffic. The air is still, and though it's only mid-morning, it's hot.

Last night Mark and Nancy Jo told me the temperature has been in the 90s down in the valley. Knowing this somehow makes it hotter here, too. In 1984 I hiked across Arizona during an unusually hot spring. I functioned fine until I met someone who told me it was 117 degrees. Everything seemed hot after that. I started to drag. When you're out in it all the time and not thinking about it, your body adjusts easily to those temperature swings that in other circumstances would be deemed uncomfortable. As I walk up the divide I wish I hadn't been informed about the heat wave.

The road offers me quick, easy travel for a few miles. I can step out with a mile-eating stride as my thoughts bounce back to the 1800s. What ever happened to the unsung heroes, the enlisted men of the expedition? I'm glad to be reminded of McNeal in Lewis's journal entry on the sign. He was one of the hunters of the expedition and is mentioned quite often. But what happened to him after those three years out here? Did he ever return to the West? Or did he come back only in his memories? Music starts flowing in my head. Each step brings another line, another note to weave an answer.

> He said, "Come with us, to the lands uncharted,
> We'll see this country at its very best,
> We'll follow the wild, wide Missouri,
> Into the sun, we'll go Way Out West."
> —from the song "Way Out West"

I'm singing as I walk. The rhythm of the new song becomes the rhythm of my step. My perspective in "Way Out West" is an overly romantic view. I know that. In fact, I celebrate that. It was a hard journey they undertook all those years ago. They didn't have the lightweight gear, the cozy sleeping bags, the detailed topographical maps. They froze in the snow. They went hungry at times. They were swarmed by mosquitoes and chased by grizzly bears. They never knew if the local tribes would want to befriend them or kill them. But I still can't help but feel that through all this, some of those men must have been touched by the wild, untraveled character of the land they explored. Some of them must have loved the wide open spaces, witnessing the land as fresh and as clean as it would ever be. Surely, some lamented the return to the East. Surely, some returned to the wilderness as their memories drew vivid pictures of that unique chapter of American exploration. My stride returns me to the backcountry, but the years lay there wondering.

I've left the road to walk the forested ridge. An old trail here has been cleared recently. The path itself is faint and indistinct, but the blazes and the route are very clear. The lodgepole pine is dense. Sometimes the trail is a tunnel through the thick wall of trees. The forest is dry. The needles crack and crunch with each step. The scent of pine is overwhelming.

The trail leads me to a benchmark where I will leave the divide, dropping down the Montana side of the mountain into Kitty Creek. As I sit in the quiet forest, enthralled by the stillness, movement catches my eye. A marten lopes from tree to tree, heading west. A few minutes later, four deer amble by. Perched there, looking up and down the trail, I'm lamenting my departure. It's been an amazing few weeks walking the Continental Divide. The sights I've seen and the thoughts I've experienced come drifting back.

I keep hoping I'll look up and see some long-distance hikers come tramping along the trail. No one comes. My rendezvous will have to come next time I walk the divide. And I know there will be a next time. The forest is still and as calm as a cave. I bid a short prayer of thanks, take a bearing on my compass, and strike off into the trackless forest.

Circle of Life

"It's a planet of blue with islands of green
Let's cherish this Life and all it means,
Each death and birth brings to this Earth
A whole circle coming clean."
                                    — *from the song "Circle of Life"*

C & L Creek. The Big Hole Divide. I'm struck by the beauty of the place. Topographical maps can show only so much. They leave out the cold morning light playing in the trees. They never mention the bird songs on the still canyon air. They neglect the creek murmuring and winding its way through the narrow canyon, or a cow and calf moose trotting up and over the hillside, deer bounding through the aspen. The place is alive. Maps don't tell you that.

The Big Hole Divide is the ridge of low mountains separating the watersheds of the Big Hole River from that of the Jefferson. It's a minor range running from the summits of the Continental Divide to the peaks of the Pioneer Range. The impacts of human activity have hit it hard. The route I'm taking attempts to skirt those impacts, searching out a pristine path among the maze of roads and extensive clearcuts.

The trail is good. The kind of trail I like to see. It hasn't been overused, nor is it worn deeply into the ground like some trails. It's narrow and faint, soft on the tread. It twists and turns through the clearings and the forest as if a deer had made it. On this morning I feel like a deer myself, stepping lightly and being watchful. I'm poking along, stopping often to listen, wandering off the path to observe. The pauses are not drawn from anything in particular, just the forest itself. It seems sharper, more defined this morning, requiring an extra look, a deeper appreciation.

The morning slips past. The little trail leads me to a wooded pass where I veer off the track to make my way up the steep, wooded slope. A well-worn elk trail, like an expressway, happens to be heading my way. An hour later I'm stepping out onto the top of Bloody Dick Peak at the crown of the Big Hole Divide. A refreshing breeze plays over the exposed summit. The cool bite is invigorating, while the sweeping panorama stretches my spirits just a tiny bit wider.

Much later, I move on, traveling a mostly forested ridge. The crest narrows for a time, marked here and there with the scars of old fires. Ghost trees bleach in the sun, hugging to the rocky crust, while new growth struggles to gain a toehold. Clark's nutcrackers flit from tree to tree, squawking and generally making more of a racket than I would prefer to have preceding me. I wish they'd hush up.

The going is slow due to the scrubby trees, jagged rocks, and precipitous drops. Marmots and pikas abound in this stretch. I expect them. I do not expect to see anything else. The nutcrackers will see to that. Besides, it's the middle of the day. Not a good time to see critters.

The ridge skirts a steep bowl that's bare of trees, laced with boulders, and almost covered with snow. I don't know why I'm so surprised. This is a north-facing slope, and I'm above 8,000 feet. Snow should be here, but with these last few days being so hot, I just haven't thought of it. I'm starting to traverse above the bowl when another patch of white catches my eye. It's more of a creamy white set against the snow. And it moves.

A mountain goat treads slowly over to the base of the bowl. He moves as if each step were an effort, as if he had just enough energy to make that one placement of his hoof. Two others lie sprawled on the tongue of snow. He joins them, plopping down as if that too were an effort. This heat today is hard on them. They're lying in the snow, panting heavily.

The average response of a mountain goat to intruders is to run. And to climb. I don't want to drive them to flight this hot day. It might kill them. I watch them for a few minutes then back off to the south side of the crest. I make my way along that side of the ridge, confident that my noise will not disturb them.

The ridge becomes broader and more heavily forested. The distant views are gone. I need my compass to tell me where I am on the mountain. I walk over an unnamed knob. Then another. The dense forest offers a cozy security and a monotony that allows my thoughts to stray with each passing knoll. I'm drawn back to that view from Bloody Dick Peak. I'm trekking miles of green tunnel, and I've got panoramas of mountain upon mountain on an endless reel playing in my mind. Beautiful mountains. Wild mountains. Mountains of the heart.

These wild mountain ranges dotting the northern Rockies *are* the heart. They are the last strongholds sheltering the living core of the region. The year's water flows from their snowfields The remnants of the last wild populations of various species dwell in their secluded reaches. The uncut forests offer sanctuary to untold numbers of organisms. Their unspoiled character shapes and directs the mood of this entire corner of the state.

The biological integrity of the area is wrapped in and woven with the health of these remaining wild ranges. A who's who list of biologists ten pages long can vouch for the importance of keeping these remote places just the way they are. Each range in the Northern Rockies still has a significant roadless area, which should be kept so. But there are other reasons besides ecological health to leave them be.

We as a species need to experience nature. Plain and simple. We need something to remind us of where we came from, something that says, "You, too, are a part of this planet." To often "nature" is but the roses in our suburban yard, or green grass in the neighborhood park. The fish in the aquarium are our only glimpse of wildlife. But they don't count. These are imitations. Pruned, fed, and pampered imitations. Nature is a living system, a living system that can stand on its own. Wilderness is nature as it was meant to be. It just is. Its birth and being do not revolve around human whims and whiles. Unfortunately, its presence in today's overpopulated world often does depend on human care. Caring enough to leave it alone.

The existence of natural areas has always been taken for granted in our society. There has always been a place for young people to go, young people of all cultures, to seek their own visions, their own directions from the spirit of the Earth. There has always been another side to the mountain. A wild side. Land "out West" to find solace and silence in. Places "up north" in which to lose ourselves and stretch our inner limits.

Today those wide open spaces continue to shrink, and with them, the visions. The neighborhood forests and fields of our childhood have been paved over or buried under by super highways and monster malls. Where will the new generation go to find a soothing connection with their own planet? Where will humankind be reminded of our own wild heritage, the animal within us? Can a child feel at home on this Earth without contact with its rhythms, systems, and fellow beings? Can life be nurtured by a computer game of virtual reality?

Reality is often a matter of perspective. The long walks and the months in the wild places have given me a wide perspective of life and where we do, and do not, fit in. I have strong opinions about how the planet should be treated. It seems to me we're watering down our quality of life with each compromise on the environmental front. We lose a bit of nature, and then we get used to it. We lose a bit more and get used to that. Soon we're living in a polluted, crowded world and we think that's the way it's supposed to be.

The strength and spiritual connection wild places hold for the human soul is a value that cannot be measured in forest plans, fiscal budgets, and biological surveys. It dwells in the very root of the Earth's existence, and thus, in ours. When we cease to have a connection with nature, and start to accept its imitations as true, we risk losing something in ourselves, a little piece of our heart. Yes, these are indeed mountains of the heart.

The ridge changes direction. Soon I'm descending a side ridge through blowdowns piled like matchsticks. I step over one log, only to climb over the next. Sometimes I balance on top, walking down one, crossing to another, and on to the next. It's slow going. Hard, too. Yet now I feel charged. I want to walk and walk. I feel like if there were more hours in this day, I could hike them. I want my brain to stop, to put my thoughts on hold. Let the swing of my stride lull me to peace. Let me forget that this wild place is but a shrinking island. Let me put aside the worries about Mom and Leslie. I just want to walk. I just want to feel the movement. And that's what I do.

For a time I slip into that trancelike travel that long-distance hikers find so helpful in passing the miles. Thought is replaced with movement. A continuous flow of muscle and bone. Step upon step. A dance. A ritual of journey as I move steadily down the gently sloping forest.

~

Today has been a short day of walking. It's just as well. The past eight miles were relatively boring miles, with many clear-cuts and much litter. Nothing like the spectacular yesterday over Bloody Dick. I could go farther today but have found a perfect campsite among big Doug firs along Swamp Creek. Besides, tomorrow I'm supposed to rendezvous with my friend Jack Kirkley for a food drop. Our meeting place is an abandoned farmhouse only five or six miles from here. I have plenty of time.

I take a bath in the creek and play my guitar for hours. Songs spill out like thought. I wander the stream bank watching birds. A porcupine scrambles up a tree at my approach. When I first arrived, deer had bolted from the trees beside the creek. This is the kind of place where an afternoon is best spent just soaking it all in. This is my life. This is what it has become. Like a sponge I absorb the moods of these wild places. I gather up the sights and smells. I collect them and store them away in my soul. Occasionally they spill back out in a song. Mostly, I just hoard their vitality. It's what keeps me going. I wonder if I should call myself a parasite.

And this leads to other thoughts today. What have I truly given this planet in return? Even living as softly as I do, I consume more than most non-Americans do. When I think about it, the only thing I have that will truly benefit the Earth is the waste I bury in a little cathole each morning. That, and my bones, which will someday sink back into the land. I'll raise one hell of a crop of bugs and microbes with this ol' body. Or perhaps a tree will tap into these minerals of mine. Maybe a gnarled, twisted whitebark pine. These are humbling thoughts, but they make me feel good. Raising a whitebark pine from the compost of this wiry body would be a noble thing.

I'm wondering about Mom again. I do that a lot. I keep trying to imagine what goes on in her mind these days. Does she ever think of things like this? Does she ever regret having us kids? Is there something she has never gotten to do? Something that facing this cancer has rekindled a desire to do? What kind of tree would she like to have her bones contribute to? I should have asked her these things this spring, but I didn't think of them until I was out here. I must ask her when I see her this fall.

The dawn is hazy and overcast. At first the sun is visible, an icy red orb peeking over the Pioneer Mountains, but in minutes the bank of dense gray clouds gobbles it up. I start out walking the stream bank but soon find myself striding along a faint, grass-covered jeep trail. This is food-drop day. I'm excited. Jack has told me he may or may not be there, but the food package would certainly be waiting for me, and I hope some word from home, too.

What seems to be level walking is actually dropping me lower into the Grasshopper Valley. It's a wide open valley with water gushing out of every fold in its sage-covered surface. I cross one rivulet after another. Waterbirds explode from the marshy spots. Elsewhere, larks and cranes abound. The air is still as a cave. The only sounds are moving water, myriad strains of birdsong, and the crunch of each step.

Four and a half miles later I'm crossing a bridge over Grasshopper Creek on a little gravel road. Up ahead are a few old farm buildings. As I get closer, they take on a melancholy tone. The two stories of emptiness seem lonely for the touch of a human hand. Most of the windows are broken. The paint is peeling. There are ghosts here. All abandoned homes have them, wisps of history, what once was, and what should still be. I can imagine children in this overgrown yard, a dad out back clanking away at something in the shed, a mom calling out to the kids to get to their morning chores.

No sign of a vehicle. Jack isn't here. A wire fence surrounding the place is down in places. I step over and into the yard. Cows have been grazing here. The big front picture window in the living room is long gone. I step over the window sill, boots crunching glass on the wooden floor. I slip off my pack and lean it against a wall. I'm moving as quietly as I can, as if not to awaken those sleeping here. That's silly, I know, but the place has presence to it. I really do feel like an intruder.

Jack has told me that my package would be propped atop a door on the upper floor. This is a place where he sometimes comes to collect owl pellets for the biology classes he teaches. I pick my way carefully up the creaking steps. The package is there, right where he said it would be. A little piece of paper is taped to it.

Removing the note, I quickly scan the words. My hands start to tremble. Leslie has called Jack with some bad news. Mom's condition has taken a turn for the worse. It doesn't look good. She's fading fast. I'll be going home. Jack is climbing Mount Baldy today, and I'm to hike up to the trailhead and meet him at his truck. He'll take me to Dillon to make some calls and then home to Big Sky.

I suppose I've known this was coming. I just didn't know how soon it would be. It's eleven miles to the trailhead. Eleven miles to the end of my trail. I'm walking up a jeep road that's getting narrower and narrower, leading me higher with each mile. That's funny: I'm heading back into the mountains, but I know I'm on my way out.

I'm walking fast. My throat is tight, and getting tighter.

A mother is a special thing. She brings you into the world, and then becomes your world. She is the source of security, the root of love, your pat of assurance, your connection to the family lines tying you to your fellow humans. My mother has been all of these to me. When I think about it, so have the wild places.

I'm thinking of the dedication I wrote for my first book of poetry, The Whisper Behind The Wind. It read, "For my mother and the Earth, one and the same." Both have nurtured me over the years. Both have taught me lessons of the heart. Both have touched me, nursed me through my troubled times. Both have always been there, a presence I could always feel, and one I could always feel a part of. I can't imagine my life without Mom. I can't imagine my life without wild places.

I'm walking faster. A tear is building in my eye.

A bumper sticker I see a lot reads, "Love Your Mother" and shows a picture of a little blue and green planet. I have loved my mother. Both of them. And now they are dying, succumbing to the cancer eating at their cores. Falling to the disease of so-called civilization. We see, and we know, but we continue to turn our heads. As if not looking will make it all better. Her systems are no longer working. Too much poison in her blood.

I'm striding as fast as I possibly can. The lump in my throat comes and goes. The jeep trail fades, becoming narrower and steeper. I know these are my last miles for this year.

Mothers represent our ties, bonds to our family, our childhood, our past and our future. I feel those strings coming unraveled. My new grief has cut me off from that nurturing peace I've been dwelling in these last weeks. I feel lost and adrift. These last miles hold no joy. I hardly see what I'm passing. My feet pound out a steady rhythm, beating into my worried heart.

I'm starting to climb out of a narrow canyon. The jeep road has become a foot trail. A sudden scream draws me to a halt, a lonesome keen, long and drawn out. It jerks me from my dreary reverie, and snaps me back to awareness. A large red-tailed hawk cries again before launching into the skies from a tall fir. As the majestic bird gains altitude, circling higher and higher on the thermals, I remember the dream of the birds and the cages. The dream that stirred me so much when I was back in the Snowcrest Range. With the memory comes a rekindling of love. It is a love that shines through grief and worry, a love that reaches into my inner core, warming me, lightening me, freeing me once again from the bars of the cage I've started to fall into.

The wind has picked up. Thunder rumbles from an oncoming bank of clouds. The sun sneaks its rays of light through a distant gap in the darkened sky, and I feel them and know that I will return. The wild places still exist. I will seek them out again, and again. This is something I must do. The sanctity of wilderness is a power that will revive me for years to come. My mother still lives. I will honor her. I will cherish her sweet memory. I will not turn my eyes away. I will face her death by her side. I will hold her close to my heart. The "Mother and the Earth, one and the same." I will stand with her, and fight for her. I will mourn her, but at the same time I will celebrate her life for what it has been, for what it is, and for what it can be.

A lightning bolt crashes to the earth a few miles away. The peaks are barely visible, ghostly outlines of rock traced in the darkest stormy blue. The scent of rain is on the wind, but I can imagine that up on those windblown slopes, far up and away, a mountain goat is somewhere ahead, somewhere on my trail, turning to see if I follow, leading the way.

Epilogue

All tales have a sequel, for life never stands still. It's always moving on, tumbling and stumbling sometimes, but always onward. That time in August is like a blur to me. Jack drove me home. I flew to Michigan the next day, but I never got to ask Mom all those questions. She died in her own bedroom on August 26th. She was sixty-two years old. I watched her take her last breath.

Biff's death in December of '91 by his own hand took another piece of my heart. No one will ever understand why such a gentle soul lost sight of himself and couldn't see the goodness we all found in him. It's been twelve years, but I still think of him often, especially those days with him on the crest of the Great Divide. He was a special man. I still meet people who met him only once but were touched by his zest and sincerity.

My friend Tom suffers now from MS. Those days in the Snowcrest Range with him and Mary are sweet memories. He doesn't get out into the wild country much these days, but he still fights for it with letters and calls. After one of my concerts in Seattle a few years ago, we were discussing the fate of some of these wild places I've written about. He had attended the concert in a wheelchair, but he turned to me and said, "Jim, it doesn't matter the fact that I can't get out there anymore. It doesn't matter if you ever do or not. The important thing is that we know that those wild places are still out there. Just knowing that, we're a little better for it. And a little stronger." And a whole lot bigger. Tom inspires me.

I still do my long treks every year. They total over 25,000 miles now. I still go solo most of the time, but Leslie has walked many a mile with me. She's still my best friend and favorite hiking partner. In 1992 I returned to the Pioneers and finished the trek I'd started in

1990, adding an additional five mountain ranges to the original loop. It turned into another 500-mile trek. That's another story.

And the wildlands? They're still there. But with each passing year more and more of them fall to development, logging, ATV abuse, road building, and human shortsightedness. The current administration in Washington, D.C., has declared war on our environment. Years of progress toward clean air, clean water, open space, wildlife, and the things that give quality to this life are being reversed. Right now is one of the darkest times for the environment, yet a few lights of hope still shine. The Northern Rockies Ecosystem Protection Act would protect all remaining roadless lands in the Northern Rockies. The wild places I've written about in this account would be kept in their present state. Adversely impacted areas would be restored to their original condition. Will we be smart enough as a species to look ahead for once? Will we have the vision to begin to walk softer on the planet?

I think that we can live side by side with delicate places and fragile species. Humans did at one time. If our ancestors were able to do it 10,000 years ago, surely we have evolved enough in those intervening years to live more wisely with the planet. We are not presently doing so, but we can. For heaven's sake (and for Earth's), let's get it together. Get out there! Listen! The wild places will fill you up. Let them.

—Jim Stoltz, January 2003

Resources

For a look at Walkin' Jim's recordings, tour schedule, photos, and more, check out his website at www.walkinjim.com. Register for his e-mail newsletter, Wild Wind, by sending an e-mail to walkinjim@ walkinjim.com.

For more information about wilderness and the environment, or to support wilderness preservation, contact the following groups: ·

Musicians United To Sustain the Environment
PO Box 671
South Lyon, MI 48178
www.musemusic.org
(Founded by Walkin' Jim Stoltz and Craig Wagner, this organization uses music to help protect wild places and wild lives.)

Alliance for the Wild Rockies
Box 8731
Missoula, MT 59807
www.wildrockiesalliance.org
(The organization behind the visionary Northern Rockies Ecosystem Protection Act)

Montana Wilderness Association
PO Box 635
Helena, MT 59624
www.wildmontana.org
(Montana's first organization dedicated to wilderness preservation)

Idaho Conservation League
PO Box 844
Boise, ID 83701
www.wildidaho.org

Predator Conservation Alliance
PO Box 6733
Bozeman, MT 59771
www.predatorconservation.org

Wilderness Watch
PO Box 9175
Missoula, MT 59807
www.wildernesswatch.org

About the Author

Jim Stoltz was born in Detroit, Michigan, in 1953. In 1974 he hiked the 2100 miles of the Appalachian Trail, walking this beautiful footpath from Georgia to Maine. The experience changed his life. Twenty-five thousand miles later he is still going strong, spending part of each year in the backcountry on his long wilderness walks. Folks just naturally started calling him Walkin' Jim after a year-and-a-half coast-to-coast trek.

When he's not out in the backcountry, Jim is often traveling the country with his concert, "Forever Wild." This multimedia program combines his live music and poetry with his photography. The U.S. Environmental Protection Agency presented Walkin' Jim with its Outstanding Achievement Award in the Spring of 1991 "for sharing nature and wilderness with others across America through your extraordinary words, images, and music." Jim has released eight recordings of wilderness-oriented music. In 1998 Jim co-founded Musicians United to Sustain the Environment, a nonprofit organization dedicated to using music to benefit wilderness and wildlife causes.

Jim currently lives in Big Sky, Montana, with his wife, Leslie.